Conducting
Productive Meetings

Conducting Productive Meetings

How to Generate and Communicate Ideas for Innovation

Teruni Lamberg, Ph.D.

ROWMAN & LITTLEFIELD
Lanham • Boulder • New York • London

Published by Rowman & Littlefield
A wholly owned subsidary of The Rowman & Littlefield Publishing Group, Inc.
4501 Forbes Boulevard, Suite 200, Lanham, Maryland 20706
www.rowman.com

Unit A, Whitacre Mews, 26-34 Stannary Street, London SE11 4AB

British Library Cataloguing in Publication Information Available

Library of Congress Cataloging-in-Publication Data Available

Library of Congress Control Number: 2018938123

ISBN 978-1-4758-4130-5 (cloth : alk. paper)
ISBN 978-1-4758-4131-2 (pbk. : alk. paper)
ISBN 978-1-4758-4132-9 (electronic)

To my wonderful parents, Kenneth and Shireen de Silva
My beloved Scott and Zack Lamberg

Contents

4 How to Communicate Effectively with Teams and Stakeholders 71

Create Mechanisms for Communication and Knowledge Sharing

*Continuous communication with immediate
feedback optimizes opportunities to innovate*

5 Moving Forward 87

Leading to Innovate Involves Continuous Learning

Preface

Innovation involves making things better, cheaper, or more efficient. It improves the human condition. An effective leader knows how to structure interactions and project meetings to move ideas forward and refine them to produce innovative solutions to problems. What sets a successful leader apart from one who just keeps things running is the leader's ability to lead a team to innovate. This book specifically addresses how a leader can structure activities and meetings to lead a team to be highly productive and innovative.

Creativity has been my lifelong passion. I have always been interested in how people become creative. I wondered: Where do ideas come from? How do creative people think and act? I studied research on creativity because I wondered how people generate creative ideas and develop innovative products. At that time, I was a teacher and explored how to produce creativity in the classroom. I wrote a master's thesis on creative thinking.

When I was hired as a postdoc at Vanderbilt University after I graduated with my doctorate in mathematics education, I found myself in the role of project manager, and very quickly realized that I needed to develop leadership skills to manage the project and generate new ideas. The whole purpose of being an academic was to make discoveries and come up with innovative and new ideas in teams.

I realized that many people come out of college with disciplinary knowledge but have no clue about how to lead a team; this included myself. It was then when I began my journey of studying research literature on leadership. The bottom line is that regardless of disciplinary learning, to make a difference requires leadership skills. Most people find themselves in this role.

When I moved to Nevada, I became the principal investigator of the Northeastern Nevada Mathematics Project, and recently, of the Nevada Mathematics Project, a statewide effort in collaboration with every school district in Nevada, Regional Training Centers, and six institutes of higher education. I have to admit that this was a massive undertaking. I knew that the success of the project depended on my leadership skills.

Therefore, I started studying business literature and research from other disciplines on how to lead teams. I found that what I learned became valuable as I led the Nevada Mathematics Project. It would have been so easy for things not to work out. Managing a team with multiple institutions and teachers spread across a state was not an easy task.

I did not have the luxury of making mistakes or not knowing what I was doing. The stakes were high; I needed to develop leadership skills to lead this project successfully. I started seeing connections between the creativity research and the business literature on leadership.

I felt the need to share what I learned because many people around the country, and even worldwide, kept asking me how I pulled this off. I embed my story throughout the book. I wanted to write a book that not only appealed to academics but also to anyone who intends to lead a team to innovate. Therefore, I present complex ideas in simple language that anyone can understand.

I was fortunate to be mentored by world-class leaders and to interview them for this book. What a privilege to share their stories and insights on how they generated ideas in meetings. Most importantly, they shared their insights on not just how they generated ideas but also the intricacies of the processes used to refine ideas and develop them into concrete theories and products.

This book documents research from my statewide research project, interviews from highly successful leaders whose work has made a national and international impact. It also contains interviews with influential K–12 leaders whose work has made an impact in their institutions. A leadership framework based on a review of research from business and other disciplines, such as creativity is described.

The larger goal of this book is to provide a practical guide to anyone who wants to lead a team to innovate. In other words, the goal is to make an impact on society. I wrote another book titled *Leaders Who Lead Successfully: Guidelines for Organizing to Achieve Innovation* that is a companion book on how to conceptualize a problem and organize for innovation. Best wishes running productive meetings to come up with innovative ideas that will make a difference!

Acknowledgments

I am thankful to everyone who inspired, encouraged, and supported me through the incredible journey of writing this book. It represents many voices, stories, and insights, which I am privileged to share. Thank you, Dr. James Barufaldi, Dr. Paul Cobb, Dr. Robert Chang, Mr. Priyan Fernando, Dr. Megan Franke, Dr. Rochelle Gutierrez, Dr. Kamil Jbeily, Dr. Richard Milner, and Dr. Mitchell Nathan for being my mentors and shaping my thinking. Your work has been innovative, making a national and international impact. Thank you for sharing your insights and experiences of leading teams to innovate.

Thank you, Mr. Dave Brancamp, Ms. Kathy Dees, Mr. David Ebert, Ms. Holly Marich, Ms. Marissa McClish, Ms. Jill Ross, Ms. Denise Trakas, and Ms. Sam Wutting. Your dedication to students is amazing, and you work tirelessly to make a difference in the lives of children. Thank you for sharing your wisdom about leading teams in a K–12 setting. You inspire me!

I would also like to thank the Nevada Mathematics Project team. What a journey to join together in a statewide effort to improve STEM education in Nevada. Thank you Ms. Peggy Lakey, Dr. Edward Keppelman, Dr. Travis Olson, Dr. Jeff Shih, Dr. Ana de Bettencourt-Dias, Dr. Barbara Perez, Ms. Tina Westwood, Dr. Rebecca Bondocco, Dr. Diana Moss, Dr. Steven Demelin, Ms. Lucy Gillette, Ms. Tina Westwood, Ms. Sarah Negrete, Ms. Kirsten Gleissner, and the Nevada Department of Education (Mr. Dave Brancamp, Ms. Tracy Gruber, Mr. Mike Pacheco, and Dr. Heather Crawford-Ferre) and Regional Training Centers (Dr. Kirsten Gleissner, Dr. Sarah Negrete and Ms. Chelli Smith) in Nevada. We were fortunate to get the support from ALL school districts in the state of Nevada and also the support of some private and charter schools. It is a privilege to work with you.

Many people read through the manuscript and provided thoughtful feedback that helped shape it. Dr. Craig Wall, thank you for helping me conceptualize this book and providing thoughtful comments throughout the writing process. Ms. Elaine Pohle provided me with critical and timely feedback. Mr. Charlie Arroyo, I am grateful for the feedback you provided from a business perspective.

I would also like to thank all the innovative leaders that I interviewed who took the time to read the manuscript and provide thoughtful feedback. Thank you, Ms. Denise Trakas, for your suggestion of including the section on K–12 voices and providing thoughtful comments. Thank you, Ms. Marrissa McClish, for your thoughts and recommendations. I also appreciate the support of Mr. Steve Harrison's group for their mentoring, especially Ms. Debra Englander, Ms. Martha Bullen, Ms. Raia King, and others. Thank you, Mr. Tom Koerner, my editor who provided support and encouraging words throughout the writing process. A special thank you to Ms. Carlie Wall and Ms. Ashleigh Cooke from Rowman & Littlefield.

I am thankful for the love and support of my parents. They live a life that involves serving others. A special thank you to my husband, Scott, and my son, Zack, who was always there for me with a warm smile and a sense of humor. I love you.

Introduction

A Framework for Conducting Productive Meetings

I begin with an idea, and then it becomes something else.

—Pablo Picasso

It was time for yet another meeting. The team members reluctantly shuffled into the room because they were required to be there. The project leader had a PowerPoint presentation and read every single slide and told the team members what they needed to know. Some team members took notes. The leader passed out several handouts during the meeting. One or two individuals asked a few questions at the end of the meeting.

Sound familiar? Have you ever sat in a meeting with glazed eyes while irrelevant information was shared? You may have found yourself secretly glancing at your phone to pass the time. People at the meeting did not share their thoughts and ideas. Attendance was taken, and a box was checked that the meeting took place. No new ideas were generated! The meeting agenda did not move the project forward. It was simply information sharing.

One might ask: "How does one lead a team to work together and come up with innovative ideas?" What does such a meeting look like? The reality is that innovation and productive collaboration do not naturally take place. The leader must structure activities and create conditions to innovate. Furthermore, each meeting and interaction should move ideas and the project agenda forward.

This book addresses how successful leaders run highly productive meetings where ideas are sparked and refined so that the meeting leads to innovative solutions to a problem. Innovation is the ability to come up with new ideas and better ways of doing things to improve the human condition. This is the reason why new products and services get developed. Our economy today is knowledge based. Therefore, innovation is an important part of advancing knowledge and improving things.

Katherine Graham-Leviss wrote an article for the *Harvard Business Review* pointing out that even though innovation is critical, it is also difficult to cultivate quality innovative leaders. Understanding how to lead productive meetings where ideas get generated and refined is an important part of being a successful leader. A leader must structure formal and informal experiences to produce the flow of ideas. The leader needs to know how to create conditions for team members to generate ideas and stretch their thinking. The leader needs to know how to capitalize on team members' ideas and lead the group into creative thinking.

Eight world-renowned researchers and a business leader who have successfully led teams to innovate and made a national and international impact share their secrets in this book. Their stories will inspire you to think of new ways to run meetings. The four leadership principles outlined in this book will guide you to make decisions to engage your team in creative problem solving.

Each innovative leader who was interviewed shared how they built a body of work over their careers that made an enormous impact nationally and internationally. Specifically, each interview covered what inspired each leader to embark on such a journey (which is documented in my book *Leaders Who Lead Successfully: Guidelines for Organizing to Achieve Innovation*), how they built a body of work over time, and most importantly, how they ran project meetings. The leaders discussed the role of formal and informal interactions and communication for innovation.

A review of research on business, creativity, and interdisciplinary research was conducted to develop the framework outlined in this book. Furthermore, the Nevada Mathematics Project, a professional development research project in the state of Nevada, is used as a case study to illustrate these principles in action. The Nevada Mathematics Project represents the beginning of a journey of transforming mathematics education in Nevada. The work is still in progress! But the project has made great strides in coming together as a state.

Understanding *characteristics* of innovative leaders as outlined in my book *Leaders Who Lead Successfully: Guidelines for Organizing to Achieve Innovation* is helpful.

CHARACTERISTICS OF SUCCESSFUL INNOVATIVE LEADERS/SCHOLARS

- *They have leadership skills and their work makes an impact in society by solving real problems.*
- *Their body of work solves a real need.*
- *They have a vision and inspire a team to act.*
- *They seize opportunities for innovation.*

- *They develop a body of knowledge over time.*
- *They have a quest for excellence.*

These characteristics are important because they influence the leaders' *decisions* and *mindset* on how they structure and run meetings and interact with teams. Most importantly, when a leader has a vision and passion, it inspires the team to act, as opposed to a leader who is simply going through the motions of leading.

Would you rather be part of a team where the leader is going through the motions of running a meeting, or would you like to be part of something exciting, new, and innovative? Most people like to be part of something exciting! A leader's passion can motivate the team to act.

The four research-based leadership principals outlined in this book will help you become a transformative leader who can structure experiences and run productive meetings to innovate. The leadership principles outlined in this book can be used in any context, not just education. It could be in a small or large setting, depending on goals and purpose. The bottom line is that these principles can be used by anyone who want to lead a team to innovate regardless of context.

- Engage in Creative Problem Solving by Capitalizing on Team Expertise
  Building on individual strengths yields creative solutions and team spirit
- The Journey of Ideas to Theory and Products Requires Action
  Teams can adapt and adjust action items to fit with project goals
- Engage in Provocative Thinking
  Opportunity to leverage resources and creatively problem solve for innovation
- Create Mechanisms for Communication and Knowledge Sharing
  Continuous communication with immediate feedback optimizes opportunities to innovate

Stories from K–12 leaders who have made significant contributions to K–12 education are shared in chapter 5 in the section titled "Voices from the Field: Innovative K–12 Leader Interviews." These leaders share insights on these leadership principles experienced in their work. These leadership principles are not limited to the field of education. They can work in any setting where you are leading a team to be productive and innovate.

HOW TO USE THIS BOOK

The purpose of this book is to help you figure out how to run highly productive meetings to innovate. Running meetings and structuring experiences that provide opportunities for creative flow of ideas is essential. Creative ideas are not enough; the leader needs to help structure interactions in order to refine ideas into innovative theories, products, or services.

Understanding the creative process is helpful. The reader will learn strategies on how to take the creative process into account when running meetings. The reader will learn strategies to help refine these ideas as a group. In addition, strategies for effective communication with the team and stakeholders is important. Specific strategies on how to do this are outlined.

Anyone who wants to lead a team to innovate will find this book useful. For example, it is intended for teacher leaders, coaches, principals, academics, program coordinators, business individuals, and others. This book is about how to make a difference by solving real-world problems and coming up with innovative solutions. The following key ideas will be addressed throughout the book:

- How to engage teams in creative problem solving
- How to run meetings to move project agendas forward
- How to consider the needs and context of how the innovation will be used by the End User to improve design
- How to effectively communicate with project teams and stakeholders

The companion book *Leaders Who Lead Successfully: Guidelines for Organizing to Achieve Innovation* addresses the following related topics and provides concrete strategies for implementation.

- How to identify a problem to solve
- How to assemble an interdisciplinary team to solve problems
- How to capitalize on the teams' expertise and strengths
- How to create conditions to generate ideas

The four leadership principles described are research-based principles for conducting productive meetings and communicating to innovate. Each principle is illustrated with examples of how world-renowned scholars lead teams to innovate as well as examples of K–12 leaders. Also, a case study of the Nevada Mathematics Project is described to illustrate these principles in action. Each chapter contains a summary of key principles, examples of these principles in action, self-reflection strategies, and action items that can be implemented right away. The book is intended to be used as a toolbox to lead a highly productive project team and to innovate.

The chapters are organized as follows: Chapter 1 is about identifying a problem or issue that aligns with the leader's vision. Chapters 2 and 3 provides strategies for structuring formal and informal project meetings to engage in creative problem solving by considering input from the End User to innovate. Chapter 4 addresses strategies on how to communicate effectively with teams and stakeholders. Detailed biographies of the innovative leaders interviewed are listed in chapter 5 as a reference. Chapter 5 contains innovative K–12 leader interviews that illustrates how the principles outlined in the book are used in a K–12 educational setting.

Several tools are provided in this book so that the ideas can be practically implemented to run a successful project. "Think About . . ." reflection questions are given throughout the chapters for the reader to reflect on their own work and make connections. The "Action Items" sections provide concrete strategies that can be adapted to lead a project team. Also, a summary of the main ideas is provided at the end of each chapter. Best wishes on your journey to leading a highly productive team to innovate.

1

How to Engage Your Team in Creative Problem Solving

It has long since come to my attention that people of accomplishment rarely sat back and let things happen to them. They went out and happened to things.

—Leonardo da Vinci

"Where do ideas come from?" is an interesting question. Ideas are products of your thoughts, experiences, and knowledge. When you make connections between your prior knowledge and new information, learning happens. Creative ideas emerge when connections are made in novel ways. Leading for innovation is more than keeping things running. It is about creating learning opportunities and making new connections to come up with novel ideas.

This book is about innovation and how to lead a team to innovate. What do teams specifically do to generate new knowledge? Many times, a team might get together to accomplish tasks, but generating new ideas and new insights is something different.

For example, if you want to clean your house, each person living there can perform a job. If everyone does what they are supposed to, you might end up with a clean house. Getting tasks accomplished is certainly easier with a team effort. If everyone completes the task assigned, the job gets done!

A team could function together to get a job completed. However, a question such as, "What does it mean to innovate?" leads to different questions such as: Can you do something better? What problems come up? Can you find a better solution? This is a different context from completing tasks to keep things functioning.

GREAT PROJECT-MANAGEMENT
SKILLS PROVIDE CREATIVE SPACE

➤ *Getting things accomplished involves figuring out tasks, assigning jobs, and monitoring to make sure the tasks are complete.*

Getting the job done involves thinking about project management. This process involves breaking up tasks into manageable chunks, assigning tasks to people, and monitoring them to ensure everything is progressing without problems. This part requires great organizational and project-management skills. Sometimes, project members need to complete mundane tasks in order to focus on more creative endeavors.

CASE STUDY: NEVADA MATHEMATICS PROJECT

There were tasks that needed to be accomplished in the Nevada Mathematics Project. The jobs that needed to be completed was to plan four week-long teacher institutes with three follow-up sessions and to conduct research. Everyone on the team was assigned tasks based on their interests and the time they had to complete them. This project required us to travel over nineteen thousand miles around the state of Nevada in a caravan of cars. Our summer institute sites in Nevada were Reno, Elko, Silver Springs, and Las Vegas.

Nevada geography is unique. It is the most mountainous state in the country with 2,167 mountain peaks, and the state is geographically large. It is the seventh largest in the nation.[1] Even though the state is large geographically, the population is very sparse. Most of the population is concentrated in Reno and Las Vegas. Rural areas have very sparse population and do not have access to regular commuter transportation and thus access to the amenities of the larger cities. The geography and the concentration of the population make communication and transportation in Nevada a challenge. Teachers in rural areas had to travel to the professional development locations as well.

Geography had to be considered when conducting a project on a statewide scale. We drove to each location in multiple cars because we had way too much equipment to transport to each location. We had our luggage, cameras, laptops, books, and other items that did not fit into a single car. Some of the tasks that we had to complete prior to each institute included ordering supplies and organizing them into boxes and folders. We needed to figure out what handouts were needed and make copies of them.

Teachers needed to be recruited, notified of acceptance, and be informed of the location of the institute in addition to the dates and times they had to be there. Building sites needed to be secured for the institutes. We had to contact different institutions to secure a location. We needed to make sure that the building was open on a Sunday, the night before the institute, to set up.

We needed to think about data collection. Someone needed to oversee videotaping and downloading the cameras and fieldnotes. We even had to figure out what we were going to do for lunch! Do we need to bring our lunch to the sessions, or were there restaurants close by? These are just a few things that needed to be organized.

Every successful project requires tasks that must be accomplished. Our project was no different. Therefore, tasks needed to be assigned, coordinated, and completed. This process involved creating checklists and assigning tasks. Each team member understood their tasks and ensured that they were completed or asked for help if needed.

Team effort was needed to get the job done. Also, an accountability system was needed to make sure everything was completed in a timely manner. Furthermore, effective communication was needed to keep things moving along.

The Nevada Mathematics Project conducted four summer institutes across Nevada. We found that we became more efficient. We knew the routine! Here is an example of a task that needed to be done and things we considered.

The task was ordering supplies for the teacher institute, as illustrated in table 1.1.

If any part of the process in table 1.1 was missing, it would have created a domino effect of frustration and disruption to the flow of the project.

➤ *Getting a job done involves thinking about tasks, people, timelines, and organizational and monitoring systems.*

Thinking about tasks, people, timeline, organization, and monitoring systems ensures that the job gets done. For example, if the supplies were

Table 1.1. Workflow of Ordering Supplies and Getting Ready for Institutes

What materials are needed?	Cost: Is it within budget?	Who is going to place the order and monitor the budget?	Where are we going to store the supplies when they arrive on campus?	Organize the materials into separate piles for each site.	Unloading and setting up at each location
The team decided on materials. Individual team members had a list of things they needed.	What is the most cost-effective way to purchase the materials? Are there cheaper alternatives? Do we need all the things on the list?	This person is also responsible for tracking and making sure the materials arrived.	Need a location to store the materials. Organized storage	We needed to organize materials so that we knew what to take to each site. What we had to do is to load our cars each week since we worked with 140 teachers. Who is going to do this so that it is consistent? Who is going to carry what in their vehicles?	When were we going to do this? Who was going to do this? How did we need to arrange the room to distribute the materials?

not ordered, it would have a domino effect on the rest of the decisions and would be frustrating during the institute because the needed supplies would not be there.

➤ *Manage time so that if a problem occurs it can be fixed.*

Managing time and anticipating problems is helpful. For example, an order placed might be backlogged, and it might take a longer time to be delivered.

CASE STUDY: NEVADA MATHEMATICS PROJECT

We encountered a backlogged order in the Nevada Mathematics Project. We had ordered supplies and only part of the order was delivered. So we had to problem solve what we could do instead.

➤ *Team members' roles need to be clearly defined so that they know what needs to be accomplished.*

➤ *An accountabilty and monitoring system is needed to ensure completion of tasks.*

Each team member had assigned tasks, and other team members monitored and checked in with each other to make sure the tasks were completed.

➤ *Create systems for accomplishing simple tasks so that it becomes a nonissue.*

For example, something as simple as a sign-in sheet can be a cause of stress. The sign-in sheets for the Nevada Mathematics Project teachers were high stakes! We needed to turn in signature sheets for the teachers to get paid. Our first year, we had a printed signature sheet. People took it to their desks and did not return it to the original location.

Many times, we would panic wondering where it had disappeared to. The solution was to get a bright-red three-ring binder that was highly visible. This way, we could spot it from anywhere in the room. We had a place for it, and people signed in as they entered and left. That way, it took away the stress of losing the sheet or the chance of forgetting it. It also kept the signature sheets organized.

This simple task became one less thing to worry about and reduced time wasted hunting for it and also stress.

> ➤ *Capitalize on the team members' strengths.*

There may be team members who have outstanding organizational skills. Linda Koyen is a very organized person. She came up with a system for filing, labeling, and organizing things. We build on team members strengths! Zachary Kirkwood, a graduate student on the project, was great with technology. He took charge of the electronic equipment.

Figuring out systems for being organized and doing things efficiently makes it easier to focus your energies on the project goals that matter. If logistics of a project are handled well, the project seems seamless and fluid. The project work looks effortless.

Project management is a critical part of running a successful project. A well-managed project is like a well-oiled machine. It can run efficiently and effortlessly. When a project is run well, it frees you up to focus on being innovative and creative. Leading a team to innovate is more than running a project well!

Think About . . .
Think about the project that you are working on:

- *What things need to be done to make sure your project is running smoothly?*
- *Make a list of all the tasks; assign them to team members based on availability and interest.*
- *Create a monitoring system for task completion.*
- *You may find that team members can come up with better ways of doing things that you may not have thought of. Build on team expertise!*

PROBLEM SOLVING HELPS GENERATE NEW IDEAS

Innovative teams engage in problem solving by identifying or thinking about a problem. They are constantly figuring out what is working, what is not, and why. They are constantly revisiting the project vision and making sure their work aligns with the project vision. The team adjusts and adapts their actions through reflection. Dr. Paul Cobb, a professor from Vanderbilt University, shares that a project team should be a "true *intellectual* community." He explains that "sometimes they are, and sometimes they are not. Ideally, you want them to be."[2]

A team that innovates is a true intellectual community. An intellectual community is driven by curiosity and by engaging in problem solving. Dr. Cobb points out that his research teams look at what is working as well as what is not working.

Sometimes the obstacles and constraints become interesting problems to solve. In his case, it became Dr. Cobb's research agenda that he has built over time. He points out that obstacles and unexpected results become a hotbed for future innovations. The obstacles and unexpected issues he encountered became the seed for the next project.

He shared that he knows other researchers who conducted research over their careers by using obstacles and unexpected issues as problems to solve. Dr. Cobb shared how his research agenda in his career was shaped by solving a need that came up as he encountered problems in a real-world context. Innovation came out of a need to solve real-world problems! Any project leader can think about obstacles or unexpected issues as opportunities to learn and innovate.

> ➤ *Being an intellectually functioning learning community is not limited to academics. Instead, any group can be driven by curiosity to solve problems and come up with creative solutions!*

Being an intellectually functioning community that engages in problem solving is not limited to academics conducting research. Any project team can become a learning community. Any group of people can be driven by curiosity, look at a problem that they are solving, and ask themselves: What is working and what is not? What can be done differently? What information do we need to solve the problem? Innovating involves defining a problem, figuring out if something is working or not, and coming up with new insights and theories.

> ➤ *Innovating involves defining a problem, figuring out if something is working or not, and coming up with new insights and theories.*

Table 1.2 captures Dr. Cobb's research thinking over his career. Figuring out what is working and what is not working drove his research agenda. What is important to be noted is that he built a body of work over time that has meaning and purpose.

Table 1.2. An Overview of Dr. Cobb's Research Agenda over His Career

Research Focus	Innovation	Obstacles Encountered	Led to Research
Classroom design experiment	Socio-mathematical norms	School board conservative versus implementing innovation	Need to consider school context and district context to implement innovation
Professional learning communities	Support teachers to learn statistics by building a professional learning community, and understand the context in which teachers teach	Differences in school contexts needed to be understood at a greater level and how to adjust when working with different settings	Need to provide insights into large-scale implementation and feedback taking the institutional context into account
MIST project Large Scale Implementation	Provide districts with feedback	The practicality of implementation	Need practical measures as tools for district leaders to support teachers

BECOME AN INTELLECTUAL COMMUNITY
THAT LEARNS FROM SHARED EXPERIENCES

An intellectual community is different from a team that simply completes tasks on a checklist. Instead, an innovative team constantly asks questions about what they are doing and if they are effective. They have a shared understanding of the problem that they are trying to solve. The team members share ideas with one another to challenge and shape group thinking. This is different from task completion and checking things off on a list! They figure out what is working and what is not. They wonder about the unexpected.

CASE STUDY: NEVADA MATHEMATICS PROJECT

The Nevada Mathematics Project team used a design research approach to professional development. This meant that we were paying attention to what was going on and adjusting to it. The whole team was in the room as the training went on.

➢ *Participation in an intellectual community is not just task completion but "active reflection" by the entire team.*

This meant that the team would adjust what they were doing during the session, based on how the teachers responded. The team members would be paying attention, listening, taking notes, and reflecting when others were presenting. This process allowed multiple lenses for analyzing what was going on.

The following example illustrates how the team adjusted and the insights that were gained. We had groups of teachers record and share their thinking on poster paper. When it was time to report on their thinking, each group hung their paper on different walls of the room. Teachers had difficulty pointing to one another's posters during the discussion because they were spread about the room.

➢ *Active reflection leads to learning new ways to do things and gaining new insights!*

We made a simple adjustment: we displayed everyone's answer on the same wall, next to each other. This simple adjustment changed the nature of the conversation. As teachers were explaining their thinking, they would naturally point to another group's poster as part of their explanation.

For example, one group explained, "We were thinking in a similar way like this group did, but we did not draw it out like this group did. So, here is our thinking." These adjustments made it easier to have a discussion that supported learning. At the end of the day, the project team would informally gather together and discuss what worked, what did not, and what we learned.

We would look at materials produced and discuss our thoughts. This allowed us to document our thinking and adjust our plans for the next day to be more responsive.

We noted that having chart papers displayed next to each other made the conversation easier because they became a tool for the discussion.

> ➤ *Group debriefing leads to powerful insights because it capitalizes on the group thinking!*

This process of brainstorming involved considering the different perspectives observed in the situation. This allowed us to have a shared understanding of the problem and adjust plans the next day.

> ➤ *The informal sharing leads to the free flowing of ideas without constraints.*

The informal sharing back and forth led to new insights. Comments would arise from the team members such as, "Oh I did not think about that. Glad, you noticed that." "What do you suggest that we do?" These informal conversations were valuable for making sense of the shared experience. Ideas and memories were fresh. This gave us an opportunity to make sense of things without the pressure of having to run the institute. It freed up thinking space for sense making. As ideas emerged, we made notes. The common experiences made it possible to discuss ideas.

Think About . . .

- *What is the value of informal interactions with team members?*
- *How does discussing things soon after a shared experience differ from waiting a couple of days to have a conversation?*

➤ *Shared experiences are organic when building on one another's experiences through reflection and action.*

Shared experience, where a team works jointly, is different from a non–shared experience, where individuals do tasks independent of each other. For example, the Nevada Mathematics Project team could have been assigned a time slot to give their presentations. They could have left the room once their part was completed.

If the team did not listen and build on one another's presentations, the professional development and the team experience would have been completely different. It would be simply checking off a "to do" list, which would have led to disjointed, segmented, and unconnected experiences for participants, instead of a connected relational understanding where the professional development helped participants make constant connections by making ongoing reference to new learning and prior learning. A project that responds to the needs of the community it serves must be reflective and a learning community. The team needs to *learn* in the process to deliver a better service or product.

➤ *An organic approach to working involves reflection and action to improve performance and to learn from the process.*

The difference between completing tasks and an organic approach to presenting tasks involves building on each other's work through *reflection* and *action*.

CASE STUDY: NEVADA MATHEMATICS PROJECT

We asked ourselves questions to help us improve what we were doing. Some of these questions included: Are we being effective in supporting teachers to learn math and science? Did the task work? Why or why not? What else could we do to improve what we were doing? We also looked at evidence of learning, understanding, partial or immature understanding, or misunderstanding.

Working to innovate involves going back and revisiting the original vision. This involves monitoring to see if we are meeting our goal. Dr. Paul Cobb would call this "testing and revising conjectures." In other words, a theory is developed, tested, and revised in action.

CASE STUDY: NEVADA MATHEMATICS PROJECT

We discovered that at times, we needed the context of science to explore the math. For example, teachers explored how shape and form affect properties of substances. They did this to figure out nanotechnology concepts. Teachers tested different sugars to see which one would dissolve faster. They conducted experiments with sugar, powdered sugar, cotton candy, mint, and ribbon candy.

This was an activity from the Materials Worlds Module developed by Northwestern Materials Research Institute. Graphing and data analysis topics fit naturally in their explanations and could support their understanding about teaching these topics further. However, we found that teachers needed to understand the mathematics at times to make sense of the science such as the Nanoscale task.

Through experience we became better at making professional decisions. For example, we became better at deciding whether to present the math task to support the science content or the science task to support the math content. As a result, we had to carefully rethink how to introduce and sequence activities. This adjustment would not have taken place if we were just going through the motions of having teachers do tasks for activities sake.

The difference between a team that innovates is the following: *The team that innovates has their "minds on." They reflect and act during this process.* Whereas a team that focuses on task completion without reflection and action does not learn. They just maintain the status quo.

The differences between these two approaches are the opportunities to learn, gain new insights, and innovate. If a team just goes through the motion of completing tasks without reflection, they are just maintaining the status quo. Sometimes task completion is necessary to get logistics done in a project. However, reflection and action is needed for the larger purpose of the project. That is to improve things. Creating optimal conditions for idea generation and innovation involves interactions between people's ideas, thoughts, materials, and even events.

Ultimately, developing a true intellectual community is about relationships and the flow of ideas, information, and knowledge between individuals. There are generally three types of interactions that take place, which include a combination of formal and informal social interactions. They are informal interactions, semi-structured interactions, and formal project meetings.

Each kind of experience affords different kinds of social interactions. The rest of this chapter will explore informal interactions. Chapter 2 will discuss in-depth additional semi-structured and formal project meetings. Relationships among the project team matters!

LAUGHTER BINDS THE TEAM TOGETHER!

Laughter is the glue that binds the team together. How do you feel when you are laughing with a group of friends? Think about the warm and fuzzy feeling you have in your heart. You may find that when you laugh, you are in a more relaxed state, and you find the experience enjoyable. Can you laugh and let your hair down with people you are uncomfortable being around?

CASE STUDY: NEVADA MATHEMATICS PROJECT

Dr. Travis Olson, who was a mathematics educator on the Nevada Mathematics Project team, and I would discuss that we knew that we were making a positive difference with the teachers when laughter filled the room. There was playful bantering going on between the teachers and us. This humor extended to how the team members interacted with one another as well.

Dr. Megan Franke, a professor from UCLA, reflected on the role of laughter. When I suggested that laughter was hard to quantify, she smiled and said, "Oh yes you can!" My curiosity was piqued!

➤ *You need to be comfortable with each other to laugh! It puts people at ease!*

INTERVIEW WITH DR. MEGAN FRANKE

The thing about laughter is, it is a shared experience. It is a shared and common experience where you must step back from the stress of it and say "yeah" I get it and we are in this together and it can be funny, and it can be fun. Right! There is something important about always remembering that we are human beings. I think that it also relieves *stress*.

➤ *Laughter relieves stress and opens people to tackle complex things.*

So, when it is stressful, and we laugh about something really stupid. We always played games with these things. But it put us in a different position with each other and equalized people in really different ways. I agree it is really, really, important!

Dr. Franke gave the example of Dr. Tom Carpenter who was a well-known mathematics educator in the field. When he was standing in front of the teachers, he made everyone feel comfortable. When there was laugher, she said that the teachers felt comfortable and were treated as equal. "But we can joke with him, and I think that it changed the game with people early on!" she explained.

THE CREATIVE PROCESS IS A PROCESS!

➤ *Laughter relieves stress induced by the creative process.*

The creative process involves a certain level of tension or stress. Think about when you are solving a puzzle; you experience a certain amount of stress until you figure it out. Sapp (1992) calls this "creative frustration." You may experience feeling uncomfortable. However, when you have that "aha" moment you feel a sense of release, elation, and even joy! Wallas's (1926) description of the creative process involves four stages:

1. Preparation: Involves consciously thinking about the problem and trying to find a solution.
2. Incubation: Allowing the mind to wonder. Not consciously thinking about the problem. (This is what happens when you are out on a walk or doing something relaxing. Thoughts are going through your head.)
3. Illumination: This is when an idea that is a solution to the problem pops into your head when you are not consciously thinking about it. (You might be taking a nap, and in the middle of it, an idea pops into your head.) You are in a relaxed state when ideas pop into your head.
4. Verification: This is when you think about the solution and make connections to the problem and verify that it is a solution. This is a conscious process.

The creative process involves being immersed in ideas, identifying a problem, and seeking solutions. This process involves consciously or subconsciously making connections in novel ways to solve a problem. Sometimes, the creative process involves redefining the problem. Most people engage in solving a problem when it is intrinsically rewarding.

CASE STUDY: NEVADA MATHEMATICS PROJECT

At various times, team members became so interested in a problem being discussed that they would spend time during and after the sessions obsessing about it or trying to come up a solution for it. They bounced ideas back and forth with the team members, looked things up, and tried things out. We chatted about it during and after the sessions.

This also goes to show how important it was to align team members' interests and expertise with the tasks they were responsible for in the project. Brilliant ideas get generated with individuals who are in a state of flow. Aligning tasks and expertise that team members find intrinsically interesting leads to a higher quality output for the project.

Charlotte Doyle wrote an article on the creative process in the *Journal of Cognitive Education and Psychology* in 2016. In this article, she explains that problem finding is an important part of the creative process. This process involves dealing with the constraints of the problem. She gave an example of a movie producer being constrained by the budget. She also pointed out those clarifying requirements to solve the problem lead to more creative outcomes.

CASE STUDY: NEVADA MATHEMATICS PROJECT

In our project, our outcome was to support teacher learning. We were constrained by time and the materials we were using. This was particularly the case when we were out in rural areas without access to additional resources. We had to find creative ways to modify and adapt our resources to support teacher learning. We also had to rely on one another's expertise and feedback.

Doyle also points out the importance of free association of ideas that one is not constrained by rule following and that leads to creative ideas. She cites Guilford, who coined the phrase "divergent thinking." She points out that divergent thinking can involve free association, but it also can involve "application of conscious strategies."[3] Understanding the creative process and the conditions for creativity is important to lead a team to innovate.

INTERVIEW WITH DR. MEGAN FRANKE

➤ *Passion and interest is an important part of creative work!*

I do think that the passion and interest in doing this work drives us all! It drives innovation, but I also think that when you are innovating with other people, that there is a *stressfulness* to it too!

➤ *The creative process is stressful due to figuring things out!*

The stressfulness is that you don't think about it the way I do, and I can't think about it to help you to see the way I think about it. I am a little frustrated about that, and you are frustrated about that.

➤ *Brainstorming with the team can be frustrating at times!*

Are we are trying to develop this coding scheme? And we don't see it kind of the same. I think that I am going to push the agenda so that it is good for the field. You think that you are pushing the agenda that is good for the field. We are talking past each other. Those conversations are really, really hard to have, and are really stressful. At least for me, they are really stressful.

➤ *Laugher, fun, and informal interactions relieve stress and enhance creative problem solving.*

I think, to be able to let off steam a little bit and to realize it is going to be okay. You are going to figure out stuff together. But it feels good, right? It feels good to laugh together a little bit and to realize that you are getting overly invested and overly narrow for no good reason. We are really good at figuring that out right now. Let people laugh a little bit. I think that is a real skill. Now, it is time to take a break, because now it leads to an enjoyable "chit chat." So, I do think that there is something about the stress of working together and trying to innovate that needs relief.

➤ *Consider the team member as a person, from a holistic perspective.*

Considering the well-being the project team creates; a supportive environment to work together. This is particularly true, especially if it requires long hours and travel away from home. Making sure that the team does not burn out, and the enthusiasm and energy level is kept up at a high level is important for productivity.

Case Study: Nevada Mathematics Project

The Nevada Mathematics Project required us to work together, play together, and travel together for four continuous weeks in the summer and for fifteen follow-up sessions during the academic year. The core team did this for three continuous years. This time commitment demanded a lot from the team. It involved being on the road, being away from families; it demanded intellectual focus and getting objectives completed.

> ➤ *Consider the human element of team members when working on a demanding project.*

There was also the physical demand of driving and staying in hotels for weeks. As a team leader, I needed to think about the *human element* of our team. I needed to honor the sacrifices my team was making to do this. I needed to think about each person's needs and their families', not just the team's. I needed to find ways to make it as comfortable as possible when we were on the road.

There were parts of the trip where our families joined us. Knowing that families were welcome made it a big adventure for them as well. We all got to know one another, not only as a team but as families. I knew that people could only perform at their peak if they were happy. If they were worried and anxious and missed their families, it would be hard to focus.

> ➤ *Turn the project into an adventure to sustain motivation and energy.*

It is one thing to be gone for a couple of days, but four weeks on the road was asking a lot of families. I had to admit, I loved having my husband and son join me for part of the trip. We drove together and got to see the beautiful scenery of Nevada. They got to go exploring and share their adventures.

By making this whole project an adventure, it sustained the team. The project motto was "people first!" This experience of having a fun and adventurous element sustained us. That means we took care of one another's health and well-being first. This also included the teachers who had given up a week of their summer vacation. If there was a need, each of us stepped in and helped.

> ➤ *Positive relationships create a great work environment.*

We became like a family. The team's interaction dynamics totally changed as we all became a learning community. A mutual respect, admiration, and love for one another developed.

> ➤ *Informal interactions create bonds and a stream of ideas exchanged in a relaxed, informal setting.*

Think About
Think about your team:

- *Do people feel comfortable with each other to express ideas freely?*
- *If not, how can conditions for trust and bonding be created so that the team can work together collaboratively?*

CASE STUDY: NEVADA MATHEMATICS PROJECT

The project team relaxed together at the end of the day. For example, when we were in Elko, we hiked the Lamoille Canyon. During this time, we admired the scenery, enjoying the fresh air, with teasing and laughter going on. Most often, the conversation at the end of the session was about what was for dinner.

During these times, we would laugh about things that happened. We all laughed at the coincidence of the team members leaving Reno at different times to arrive in Elko. The driving distance from Reno to Elko is about 288 miles. However, we all managed to stop at the restaurant called the "PIG" in the city of Winnemucca at the same time. This was not part of the plan! Winnemucca is a city located about halfway between Reno and Elko. Some of us had obviously driven faster, while others decided to stop and explore on the way!

> ➤ *Informal interactions lead to timely free flowing of ideas and brain-storming.*

During our informal interactions, we would discuss something that we had observed that day. We would think about what the data was telling us. At that moment, decisions about what to do the next day would be changed based on the discussion as new ideas got generated. There was no formal agenda other than to relax and have fun. These experiences allowed us to develop real friendships and get to know each other at a personnel level. We knew what each person ate, what their likes and dislikes were, and their personality quirks.

Sometimes, there were team members who liked their quiet time. We respected that. These social interactions were valuable for opening the free flow of ideas. When we were in the sessions, we could give constructive feedback and express our opinions honestly. The dynamics of interaction had evolved from our initial project meeting when the team members' interactions with each other were a little more formal. Now, we were very were comfortable with each other. This comfort level allowed us to function as a team over the sustained period.

FRESH IDEAS ARE GENERATED FROM INFORMAL EXCHANGES

The experience of working and having fun together was not just unique to the Nevada Mathematics Project. Dr. Cobb mentioned that his MIST project required his team to travel together for four weeks too. He pointed out that they stayed at the same hotel and ate together. He said, "A lot of conversations, ideas, and things happened there." He pointed out that different kinds of information were shared in these informal interactions than at the formal project meetings.

INTERVIEW WITH DR. PAUL COBB

The conversations are more *generative* when you are traveling around. Some ideas emerged when conducting interviews, they are more "what if, and I wonder. . . ."

For example, one idea of leadership came out of interviewing one day about six or seven district leaders back-to-back. Some of the differences were striking. If more data collection than doing analysis. It was more doing stuff, it can be perceived as something later and lead to research questions.

A lot of these ideas that come out might be half baked. Because they are more "what if you want your research questions to come out of stuff?" Like, "what did the district leaders say they are doing?"

Dr. Megan Franke also pointed out that some of the most valuable conversations happened in the car as she and her team were traveling after collecting data. After you have engaged in work together, your ideas are fresh, and you are in a relaxed state. This creates conditions for the free flowing of ideas.

INTERVIEW WITH DR. MEGAN FRANKE

Sometimes our project meetings are conversations in the car after we just collected some data. We would be debriefing about what we think happened at the moment, and what we all noticed. And worries we have about the data that we just collected. And what we are excited about.

These spontaneous informal exchanges are a valuable part of generating ideas. The team is removed from the stress of running a project. Furthermore, there is a temporal element. This means a shared experience just occurred, and it is fresh in everyone's mind. There is a temporal element in this experience. If the team has had their "minds on" during the experience, ideas get shared naturally because the mind wants to make sense!

There is no pressure to produce something in this context. The body is in a more relaxed state. The pressure to preform by running something is not there. If the same individuals met a week later as opposed to immediately after, the conversation would be very different. Most people would not remember the nuances of that day. Furthermore, if team members were not intellectually engaged during the activity, chances are the informal interactions would not be beneficial to advance ideas.

The relaxed state is the incubation state that Wallas (1926) had outlined as part of the creative process. So, it makes sense that when people are relaxed, they are engaged in free association without constraints.

Think About . . .
Think about a project that you are working on with your team:

- *Spending a little time after the project activity to debrief in an informal setting is helpful. This might include having a cup of coffee or having dinner together. It could be as simple as taking a walk. But the key is that it is something that is relaxed and not forced so that ideas can flow freely.*
- *If the conversations are forced, the flow of ideas will likely be different.*
- *Jot down thoughts. Perhaps they might be written on napkins or recorded on a phone when new thoughts are triggered. These types of interactions can spark new ideas.*

RETREATS ARE POTENTIALLY HOTBEDS FOR CREATIVITY

➤ *Find an optimal physical environment such as nature or another place that inspires your team to be creative.*

Think about a time you were out in nature or a place that just inspired you. Jot down your thoughts in a journal. Why were you inspired to think and reflect? What did you experience and feel? What ideas popped into your head? What is your dream environment in which to be creative? What would it look like, smell like, and feel like? Is it the ocean breeze on your face or the cool mountain air? What is your ideal space to be creative?

CASE STUDY: NEVADA MATHEMATICS PROJECT

> When we hiked in Lamoille Canyon, we were so inspired by the majestic mountains of Nevada. It was a spiritual experience. Dr. Mathew Hsu (a scientist on the project team) whispered that you could feel God's presence here. "How can you not be thankful?" We experienced the rush of the cool summer breeze on our faces, the rugged terrain filled with wild flowers, and a bubbling stream.

> The smell of the damp earth under our feet was intoxicating. We were climbing a mountain, just as we had in our sessions. We were a team; we were watching out for each other. Each person noticed something beautiful in the formation of the rugged terrain. Perhaps it was a plant that we had not seen before. We were climbing the mountain together. We were working toward a higher purpose. We were connected.

The environment enhances your creative ideas' flow. It builds team spirit. If you were in a loud and noisy place with constant interruptions, it would be very hard to think. Creativity requires a space where you can be quiet and have time to think and where ideas can incubate. Mihalyi Csikszentmihalyi, the author of *Creativity: Flow and the Psychology of Discovery and Invention* (1996), points out that the physical environment affects feelings and thoughts. He points out that even though there is no scientific proof, many cultures believe that the physical environment matters.

CASE STUDY: NEVADA MATHEMATICS PROJECT

> We found that our experiences of hiking together, being out in nature, created a relaxed state of happiness and well-being. In addition, it connected us as a team. We could feel the difference when we were outdoors relaxing and hiking. We engaged in deep philosophical conversations that naturally emerged.

Several leaders that I interviewed organized retreats for their team to reflect and write and come up with ideas and products. A project team needs time to step back and reflect without being constrained by having to do work, in other words, project-related work such as running a professional development session.

Retreats provide opportunities for reflecting on cumulative experiences. They are also opportunities to brainstorm and refine ideas as a team, to think in novel and creative ways. Retreats can be a reminder, or bookmark of sorts, to build in time and "space" to think.

Dr. Franke described the retreats that she and her colleagues engaged in.

INTERVIEW WITH DR. MEGAN FRANKE

We used to name our meetings by where we went. For example, if we were meeting at the National Council of Teachers of Mathematics (conference) we would add a couple of days and meet together. We went out of the city and rented a three-bedroom place, where we could cook, walk and write and do those things together.

➢ *Finding optimal physical locations that can generate creative flow of ideas is helpful.*

Some of our best conversations were when we cooked, and we ate together. It brings out other people's expertise. Like Angela, my senior researcher and previous doctoral student, is the most amazing cook! It opened up a space where she was comfortable and then could easily add to our substantive conversations.

➢ *Gathering around informal shared experiences provides opportunities for bonding and chatting.*

And it positioned her in a really different way that made the other part of her participating really a little bit easier. She could do all these cool things and we learned this other thing about her. I would say even though it might have looked like having these parts of down time. *It was the most important time for our work!*

➢ *Physical activity and reflection allows for creative flow of ideas.*

Take a walk on the beach together, or sometimes it was walk and talk, and sometimes it was less walk and more talk. It was always about figuring out how to work together.

So, for ours, we never met for a week, it was a little bit of luxury that we could not figure out how to do. We always met for two nights. We have at least two dinners together, and two breakfasts together and we always try to find some place that was not in a city. (In a downtown kind of area.) That was part of the preference of this group.

➤ *Working and playing together lays a great foundation to build on.*

We worked!! We would practice and rehearse together. We would give each other feedback. We would talk and re-write articles together. And, we would work through the details of an outline and coding. We could get enough of it done in person that it just supported the rest of the conversation that we were going to have.

Not only did Dr. Franke organize retreats, but Dr. Nathan Mitchell, a professor from the University of Wisconsin at Madison, also did as well.

INTERVIEW WITH DR. NATHAN MITCHELL

One thing we did that was great was that every year, in May, I was in Boulder at that time, . . . every May. We would meet at a mountain retreat center in Estes Park for a like a week. And, people would bring kids and their spouses. It was such a nice place to go, and we would have these day-long sessions of which we structured and composed of in various forms.

The theme that emerged is that *nature* is a powerful place for *reflection*. When people gather together in a relaxed setting, it allows for the creative flow of ideas. It binds people together around common experiences. Free-flowing conversations, as well as idea generation and refinement, take place.

➤ *Nature is a great place for people to unwind, connect with each other, and allow the incubation stage of the creative process to take place.*

The organized retreats are informal and have some structure. The team gets together with specific goals in mind such as to write a paper together, or create a coding scheme. There are goals, but flexibility too. The teams get to interact with one another as people, develop friendships, relax, and unwind together. This allows the incubation stage of creativity to take place to attend to ideas and tackle problems that were sometimes stressful to solve.

CHAPTER SUMMARY

Engage in creative problem solving by capitalizing on team expertise. *Building on individual strengths yields creative solutions and team spirit.*

A team that innovates is a team that functions as an *intellectual community.* Members have their "minds on" as they participate in the project. They are constantly thinking, questioning, reflecting, adapting, and changing. Their participation is generative. In other words, the team members bounce ideas off one another to brainstorm new ideas. Most of the conversations are about problems they are solving. They constantly think about "what works" and "does not work."

In contrast, a non–intellectually functioning group simply completes tasks independent of one another. Their goal is to complete tasks on a checklist to get the job done. There is little deviation from the plan or communication with each other. Following rules and procedures guides their plan of action. They are not open to new ideas or new ways of doing things. This type of group maintains the status quo and does not generate innovative ideas. Sometimes, this type of interaction is necessary to get objectives of a project accomplished.

A team that innovates is usually involved in some project and is constantly thinking about the problem they are trying to solve. Project management to get the tasks done is important to free up space for ideas to be generated. There are many kinds of interactions that take place among team members.

Informal interactions are important for the creative flow of ideas. The creative process involves thinking about a problem, and coming up with a solution. The incubation stage is an important part of generating creative ideas. The creative process can be rewarding when a solution is found, but during the process it can be intense and stressful.

That is why it is important for the team to bond and feel comfortable so that they can discuss and work through ideas, even if they don't always agree or are not on the same page. This is part of the creative process. Informal interactions allow the team to bond and communicate with free-flowing ideas. The next chapter will explore semi-structured and structured meetings for creativity and innovation. Table 1.3 illustrates the difference between an intellectual community and non–intellectually functioning community. Table 1.4 provides an outline of project management ideas and Table 1.5 provides strategies for engaging in creative problem solving.

Table 1.3.   The Difference Between an Intellectually Functioning Community and Non-Intellectual Functioning Community

AN INTELLECTUALLY FUNCTIONING COMMUNITY	A NON–INTELLECTUALLY FUNCTIONING GROUP
• "Minds on" constantly reflecting and revising	• Focuses on task completion as a checklist
• Engage in shared experiences	• Not reflective
• Share ideas with each other	• "Minds off"
• Give each other feedback	• Does not communicate
• Brainstorm together	• May not experience shared experiences
• Challenge each other's thinking	• Focus on getting tasks done
• Accomplish task but connect to theory of what is working or not	• Does not adapt or deviate from plan
• Is adaptive	• Not open to new ideas, "this is the way we do things."
• Seeks to understand "what is working or not"	• Follows rules as guidelines
INNOVATES/GENERATIVE	COMPLETES JOB

TABLE 1.4: PROJECT MANAGEMENT
GETTING THE JOB DONE!

TASK: Identify tasks that need to be accomplished.

- Break down larger tasks into smaller chunks and assign specific tasks to team members.
- Create a checklist to ensure the work is completed.

TIMELINE: Prioritize tasks.

- Figure out due dates for work completing and prioritize!
- Identify workflow sequence. Which tasks needs to be completed in what order to keep the work flowing.
- Manage time by prioritizing work.

PEOPLE: Assign tasks based on skill, expertise, and availability.

- Provide specificity of tasks to be completed and timelines.
- Match tasks with expertise.

MATERIALS: Identify materials and supplies needed.

- Consider budget
- Storage
- Organization and access

BUDGET: What is your budget? How are you keeping track?

LOGISITICS: What are my systems for keeping track of things: organizing systems such as labeling, filing, storing materials, communication modes, and so on.

MONITORING SYSTEM: How are you managing people, holding them accountable, and keeping track of things. Come up with a system that works for you.

EFFICIENCY: Explore if there are ways to make your tasks more efficient.

TABLE 1.5: STRATEGIES FOR ENGAGING IN CREATIVE PROBLEM SOLVING

Building an Intellectual Community

- Innovating involves defining a problem, figuring out if something is working or not, and coming up with new insights and theories.
- Shared experiences are *organic* when building on each other's experiences through *reflection* and *action*.
- You need to be comfortable with each other to laugh! It puts people at ease!
- Laughter relieves stress induced by the creative process.
- Consider the team member as a person from a holistic perspective.
- Find an optimal physical environment such as nature or another place that inspires your team to be creative so that ideas can incubate.
- Informal interactions create bonds, and a stream of ideas is exchanged in a relaxed informal setting.

Fresh Ideas Generate from Informal Exchanges

- Informal sharing leads to the free flowing of ideas without constraints.
- Shared experiences are organic when building on each other's experiences through reflection and action.
- An organic approach to working involves reflection and action to improve performance and learn from the process.
- You need to be comfortable with each other to laugh! It puts people at ease!
- Laughter relieves stress and opens people to tackle complex things.
- Laughter relieves stress induced by the creative process.

Retreats Are Potentially Hotbeds for Creativity

- Find an optimal physical environment such as nature or another place that inspires your team. Nature is a great environment for people to unwind and connect with each other and allow the incubation stage of the creative process to take place.

The Creative Process

- Be immersed in ideas.
- The creative process involves identifying a problem and seeking solutions by trying to make as many connections between knowledge and experiences in novel ways.
- A possible solution might emerge to the problem. And it may involve redefining the problem.

NOTES

1. Appendix B: Nevada Geographic and Demographic Data, Nevada Aging and Disability Services Division, http://grant.nv.gov/uploadedFiles/grant nvgov/Content/Research/Appendix%20B.NevadaGeographicandDemographicData.pdf.

2. Interview of Dr. Paul Cobb conducted by Teruni Lamberg.

3. Nevada Mathematics Project was a statewide initiative led by Teruni Lamberg who served as the Principal Investigator to support teachers to improve instruction in mathematics and science and conduct effective ways to support teacher learning. The project was awarded by the Nevada Department of Education with Math and Science Partnership Funding from the U.S. Department of Education. The project team consisted of partnership with six institutes of higher education, regional training centers and every single school district in the state of Nevada including some private and charter school. Details about this project and the team members are available in the Nevada Mathematics Project website: http://www.nevadamathproject.com.

2

How to Run Meetings to Move the Project Agenda Forward

You are today, where your thoughts have brought you.
You will be tomorrow where your thoughts take you.

—James Allen

Everything begins with an idea! How does one turn ideas into theories, services, or innovative products that can potentially make an impact? Have you ever come up with great ideas and insights but never had time to act on them? Action is required to keep things moving forward to make a difference. A project leader needs to create conditions for generating and refining ideas. The goal is to come up with better ways of doing things, such as developing new theories, products, or services.

A single idea can lead to multiple ideas. Developing ideas and refining them leads to theories, services, and products. Sharing ideas with others is necessary for implementing them to make a difference, states John Maxwell (2011). The process of innovating involves developing creative solutions, products, or theories to improve things. This process may not always involve a linear path. Innovation takes place when a problem is solved in a novel way and improves things.

The idea-development and refinement process involves interactions among people, events, and tools. A community of practice is a group of people working together on a common purpose called a *joint enterprise*. To do this, they use tools and communicate with a shared language.

A community that innovates works toward the common purpose of solving a problem. How people participate in the project team may be different based on the situation. Not everyone can meet face-to-face all the time.

The common purpose of the Nevada Mathematics Project was to increase teachers' content and pedagogical knowledge of math and science. We wanted to support teachers to help their students learn. The team was spread out across geographic regions. Sometimes different groups met at different times, based on need.

Time constraints, budgets, and geographic locations influence how people participate and interact with each other. Therefore, carefully consider how the team can gather to share ideas and generate new ones. Think about how to structure the project meetings.

Think About . . .

- *Why do you need to meet?*
- *How often do you need to meet?*
- *When do you need to meet?*
- *Who needs to meet?*
- *What needs to be accomplished*

FREQUENT, FORMAL, AND INFORMAL
INTERACTIONS LEAD TO SHARED UNDERSTANDING

➤ *The frequency of interaction influences the dynamics of the conversations.*

How often the team meets influences the kind of information that gets shared and the opportunities for exchanging ideas. When a team meets regularly, a lot of ideas get exchanged back and forth. When this happens, everyone is on the same page when conversations occur.

When project team members frequently communicate with one another, a unique communication style develops within the group that outsiders may not understand. These conversations lead to a shared understanding. Therefore, there is no need to keep clarifying things. The team can dive right in and get to work.

How the team interacted over the four weeks of traveling and working together evolved. The first week of the summer institute, the team was listening and reflecting on one another's presentations. We had an idea of what the project might look like based on the planning meeting. However, we had not seen the others present just yet. Therefore, we had to experience what each one was thinking.

We were just beginning to understand the others perspectives on things. Once we had this shared experience, our communication evolved. We no longer needed lengthy explanations to understand each person's thinking. We could simply get to the point. For example, when we talked about the "Geyser task," everyone knew what we were talking about. This type of communication freed up mental space to think about other things.

Pretty soon we were finishing each other's sentences. We understood how the others were thinking! We had become a *learning* community, and were functioning synergistically as a team. This type of communication is a luxury and may not always be realistically feasible.

MOTIVATE THE PROJECT TEAM

➤ *A collaborative project agenda is needed to come up with ideas.*

The team must be willing to work together. Dr. James Barufaldi, former director of the Center for STEM Education at the University of Texas at Austin, pointed out that the leader must make it clear to the team that this is a required expectation. He explained that it is important that the team understand that "we are going to figure things out together."

INTERVIEW WITH DR. JAMES BARUFALDI

You must have the right people on your team. By that, I mean those that believe in what you and others are attempting to do. You can't have those outliers or those "naysayers." It is crucial to have the right people on your team.

Some of the most successful research teams that I have been on—they always brought in quality people who believed in the improvement of quality biology education. They came from all disciplines. . . . I think the key is to select the right people who are open to new ideas. They don't come in with a hidden agenda. They come in with a *collaborative* agenda.

What Dr. Barufaldi is emphasizing is the difference between a *fixed mindset* and a *growth mindset*. People with a fixed mindset are not open to ideas, whereas people with a growth mindset believe that they can learn new things and are open to new ideas. Carol Dweck (2006) wrote the book *Mindset: The New Psychology of Success,* where she explains the difference between these two types of mindsets. You want people on your team who are learners and open to new ideas. People with a fixed mindset make it difficult to innovate because they are unwilling to learn.

> ➤ *Tangible products that yield individual successes motivate the team to produce.*

Providing opportunities so that individual team members can benefit personally or professionally motivates them to do their best. There should be some rewards that can help them advance their careers and make a difference.

Dr. Nathan points out that incentives such as a need for publication for tenure and promotion are motivators for people to put in the effort. He also notes that these products also came with deadlines that move the agenda forward. Therefore, you need to think about giving people opportunities to be successful. The need to generate products or solutions motivates people to put in the effort.

This means that the team must work toward developing tangible products that are meaningful to them personally as well as the team. Dr. Barufaldi explained the importance of having something tangible to work toward.

Interview with Dr. James Barufaldi

As a leader, you must give everyone the opportunity to be successful. There must be something in it for everyone. I have been on research teams where people would ask, "What is in it for me? Why should I do this? I am doing this extra work. There is no incentive. . . . "

The more I think about it, you need to know what each member is going to get out of it. A research paper, a collaborative paper, a promotion? You must understand what they are getting out of it, if you are building this team.

TAKE TIME TO THINK AND REFLECT WITHOUT DISTRACTIONS

Strategically structured project meetings can play a significant role in innovation. Project meetings are opportunities to share ideas, generate new ones, and come up with creative solutions and products. The following section provides examples of how different innovative leaders structured project meetings. These examples are helpful to think about how to structure meetings to innovate.

There are two types of meetings. Project action meetings involve figuring out how to structure the work of the project. For example, the Nevada Mathematics Project planning meeting involved a team coming together to thoughtfully design a project, assign tasks, and lay out a plan. Whereas in a project reflection meeting, the team is able to step back and reflect on the work.

Retreats provide opportunities for informal structured, semi-structured, and formal interactions to take place. The important point about retreats is that the team is not focused on doing the work of the project, such as teaching summer institutes. Rather, it is a time for the project team to step back and think about what they have been working on and how to move forward.

Reflecting without distractions eliminates the pressure from working on the project. It is time for the project team to *think, reflect, revise,* and *extend* their thinking so that the team moves toward the project goal of solving a problem. Stepping back and reflecting eventually leads to the development of theories and products. Have you ever had experiences where you were so busy "doing" that you did not have time to think about "what" you were doing and even "why"?

Having time to think is something many people from different disciplines recommend. People just need time to think and reflect. Set aside time for you and your team to just think about what you are doing. Dr. Mihalyi Csikszentmihalyi, the author of *Creativity*, points out the importance of being able to concentrate without distractions for ideas to flow.

The team needs to be immersed in ideas to be able to create. They need to be able to lose themselves in their thoughts without worrying about getting other things done. Retreats provide uninterrupted time to think. Therefore, structuring experiences to optimize thinking is needed. The following section delves deeper into how different innovative leaders structured their retreats and project meetings.

PROJECT MEETINGS SHOULD DRIVE THE AGENDA FORWARD

How team members participate in a project is influenced by time constraints and geographic distances and other demands on their time. Semi-structured and structured meetings are helpful to move ideas forward. They force the team to come together to flush out ideas and reach a shared understanding as a group.

A semi-structured meeting is where there is a set agenda for part of the time. The rest of the meeting is free flowing. A structured meeting has an agenda planned for the duration of the meeting. Either format works, depending on the context that makes sense. The goal of project meetings should be to share, generate, and refine ideas. The structured activities in a project meeting must be flexible and adaptable to meet the session goals.

> ➤ *A team that innovates focuses on ideas and is flexible and open to new possibilities and connections as opposed to following a rigid agenda with fixed predetermined rules.*

MOVE IDEAS FORWARD THROUGH DISCUSSION

Each project meeting should focus on discussing a problem or issue that the team is trying to solve. At the end of the meeting, new insights and understandings related to the issue discussed must be reached as a group. Each team member should have the opportunity to share their thoughts, listen to one another's perspective, and provide input to shape the thinking of the group. This process should lead to innovative thinking and creative solutions.

Start meetings by stating a problem and engaging the team in a dialogue. Figure 2.1 represents the movement of ideas that needs to take place in the project meetings.

The Three Levels of Sense-Making Framework (see Figure 2.1) for Project Meetings protocol is helpful to move ideas to more refined ideas. This process is not just limited to research teams. Any project team that is working together to make things better can use this protocol regardless of context. It is easy to use and moves thinking forward. The project can be large or small, it does not matter. The context or discipline does not matter!

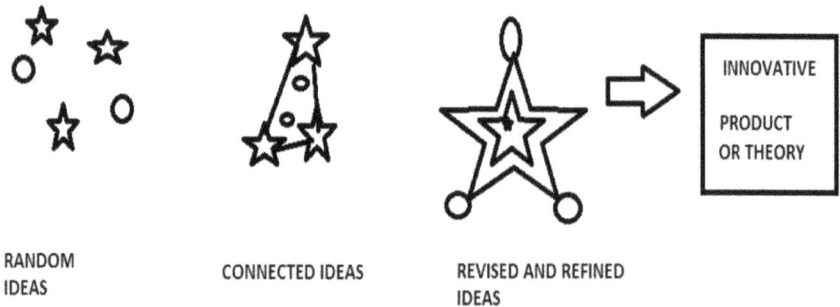

RANDOM IDEAS   CONNECTED IDEAS   REVISED AND REFINED IDEAS   INNOVATIVE PRODUCT OR THEORY

Figure 2.1.   The Journey of Ideas into Knowledge and Products
Teruni Lamberg

TABLE 2.1: THREE LEVELS OF SENSE-MAKING FRAMEWORK

LEVEL 3: FIND COMMON GROUND, NEW INSIGHTS AND IDENTIFY ACTION ITEMS
- Record themes that emerged from the conversation
- Identify new insights and knowledge related to the problem discussed
- List action items to move project forward

LEVEL 2: ANALYZE, COMPARE AND CONTRAST IDEAS
- Analyze each other's ideas shared
- Look for similarities and differences
- Brainstorm new ideas

LEVEL 1: SHARE THINKING AND UNDERSTAND OTHER PERSPECTIVES
- Ideas and information are shared
- Group listens and asks clarifying questions

Lamberg, Teruni, *Whole Class Mathematics Discussions: Improving In-Depth Mathematical Thinking and Learning,* first edition, ©2013. Reprinted by permission of Pearson Education, Inc., New York, New York.

First Level of Sense-Making: Share Thinking and Understand Others' Perspectives

When people get together, it helps to hear others' thoughts and ideas about a problem or issue. Providing a meeting agenda ahead of time is helpful for the team to prepare for the meeting. The goals of the meeting and the problem to be addressed and must be made clear.

To get people focused on the problem at hand, pose a question and ask individuals to share their ideas and perspectives. The goal is to understand different points of view. Clarifying questions can be asked if something is unclear. The goal is to exchange ideas and learn about each other's thoughts about the issue and reflect on one's position.

Second Level of Sense-Making: *Analyze, Compare, and Contrast Ideas*

This level of discussion should involve analyzing one another's thinking by looking for commonalities and differences. This is a powerful exercise because it involves critically thinking about others' thinking. The team is not just passively listening. Instead, they are reflecting and shaping each other's thinking. Multiple connections can be made through reflection.

➤ *Third Level of Sense-Making*: *Discover Common Ground, New Insights, and Identify Action Items*

The third level of discussion should involve finding "common ground." It is helpful to record the ideas that emerge in the project meeting. This written document is valuable at the end of the session to verify if everyone is on the same page. The document can be further analyzed to explore how it relates to the project goals. End the meeting by identifying action items to move the project forward. The end of this chapter contains a list of questions to support the Three Levels of Sense-Making Framework for Project Meetings to move ideas forward.

An innovation matrix can be created by the project team to articulate what they are trying to accomplish and what actions should be prioritized. An innovation matrix is a grid that lists the initiatives across two dimensions—external opportunity and internal capability. Initiatives that have high capability and high opportunity represent low-hanging fruit, which get prioritized.

Initiatives that have low opportunity and low capability represent "moon shots" and are at the other end of the spectrum. Initiatives in the middle will need to be prioritized by weighing the odds-on strength of capability versus the opportunity. Bransi Nagji and Geoff Tuff (2012) wrote an article in the *Harvard Business Review* titled "Managing Your Innovation Portfolio." They emphasize the importance of being clear about what the team is trying to accomplish and plans for innovation. Once there is a clear idea, then a matrix can be created to identify criteria and success toward the goal.

When conducting a project meeting, it is important to consider the big picture of what you are trying to accomplish. Team members must be mindful that they are not just cutting stones but building a cathedral. Conducting meetings to innovate must involve a design process.

Many fields such as engineering, education, and business use design research to test and refine innovation. This process involves designing something, testing it out, and revising it multiple times to make it better. Project meetings can use this approach as well. Dr. Cobb shared the design approach he uses in his meetings.

DESIGN APPROACH TO
MEETINGS HELPS IMPROVE AND REFINE INNOVATION

➤ *Structuring what people are presenting with templates is helpful to sharing information.*

Dr. Cobb starts the meeting by sharing with his team the goals of the project, and what the team hopes to accomplish in the meeting. He clarifies each person's role and action items. Prior to the meeting, he sends clarifying documents so that people come prepared to share what they are working on.

Team members usually prepare slides and send them to him ahead of time. Thus, he structures the meeting by having team members prepare ahead of time. Dr. Cobb shared that giving the team a template helps. For example, he asked his team to think about and answer the following questions to prepare for meetings:

- What research questions are you investigating?
- What are you analyzing?
- What did you do? Why did you do it? And, what have you found?

Preparing ahead of time leads to a more efficient meeting. Dr. Cobb explained that it was only after the team members had shared their thoughts that they would receive feedback from the group. Therefore, the team was expected to listen to one another's explanations.

> ➤ *Project meetings can be treated as an iterative design process of testing and revising conjectures.*

Dr. Cobb noted that figuring out what is not working is just as important as knowing what is. The issues of what did not work lent themselves to further investigation and became part of his research agenda. He explained his thinking process for conducting project meetings.

- Dr. Cobb shared that his goal was to make sure that everyone understood what they were trying to figure out. Everyone on the team needs to understand the goals of the project and what they are trying to accomplish as a group. This way, they see the connection between the piece they were working on fitting in with the bigger picture. He would ask everyone to share what they were working on and their current thinking about the issue. (*First Level of Sense-Making*)
- The project team works together on the same problem. However, each person focuses on a part. In the project meeting, Dr. Cobb poses questions so that the team can see connections between the pieces they are working on and the rest of the team as it relates to the problem. (*Second Level of Sense-Making*)

> ➤ *Only provide relevant feedback so that it is useful.*

- Dr. Cobb felt giving feedback is useful only if it is relevant. When people share, others can ask questions. Dr. Cobb shared that the goal of his meetings are to develop a "theory of action." The meeting that he described involved getting the team together to create a book. Each team member would contribute different chapters. By defining the product, the team knows the goals of the project. The goal is to come up with an innovative product. Therefore, there was a purpose for working on the parts.

The goals of the project meetings were about "testing and revising conjectures in a principled way."

- The team came up with theories of what worked or what did not work. Then they would test it out. At the end of the project meeting, the group would refine or create new conjectures and come up with action items to move things forward. (*Third Level of Sense-Making*)

The important takeaway from what Dr. Cobb described is the design process at work. Each meeting was about testing, and refining the design of what they were doing and documenting ideas that were generated. They used an iterative design process of testing and revising conjectures. Any project team regardless how big or small, or discipline, can engage in this type of thinking.

The big takeaway from this chapter is to always connect the pieces that you are working on to the "bigger picture" of what you are trying to achieve. Articulate what is happening or not happening and why. You need to move ideas toward your team's end goal. Scott Belsky (2016), the author of *Making Ideas Happen*, points out that when creativity is combined with our ability to stay organized, an impact can be made. However, if creative ideas are generated but are not organized, then there is very little impact. The ability to organize and keep things moving toward project goals is critical.

➤ *Living documents capture team thinking in moments of time.*

As your team generates ideas, those ideas must be captured in written form so that they can be refined. Part of this process involves managing and coordinating information. The other part is about making connections and pushing the boundaries of thinking.

When ideas are recorded in the Nevada Mathematics project meeting, they can become a tool for reflecting and having a conversation. The team may have shared multiple documents or even generated multiple reports at the meeting. However, synthesizing everyone's thoughts into a single document is helpful. The key findings are made explicit and manageable. Additional information can be added to this document over time to keep track of the project thinking. Dr. Cobb shared that at the end of the meeting, they aim to produce something concrete.

Dr. Cobb said that "we put a document together as a point of reference." The document becomes a living document at that moment in time that captures the thinking of the group. This document becomes a focal point of conversations, and that becomes refined over time.

➤ *Document what the group is thinking, not just doing.*

The important part that Dr. Franke pointed out is that the document must capture what the team is thinking, not just doing. Dr. Franke illustrates what this looked like in her project.

INTERVIEW WITH DR. MEGAN FRANKE

How to keep track of where you are and what is important as a group. *Not just what has been done but what we are thinking?*

➤ *A tool can become the living document that conversations are focused around.*

So, what are tools that we are using to help us to manage the work? What do we think about it? So, in some of my groups, it is the code book. The code book serves as a place for where we elaborate in all our notes and documents what we are thinking and what we are not sure about, and where we are with that idea. It is all being written down in the code book.

➤ *Tools can keep track of historical conversations just like the living document.*

It's all in one place and all in relation to one another. . . . If we put it here in the code book, it is front and center every time. Whatever ways that the groups have, keep track of where we are in our thinking at this moment. It is in our research group, and so we see it all the time.

➤ *Tools can remind the team about thinking in a moment in time.*

We talk so much to each other, we don't need as many tools to remind ourselves where we are at in our thinking.

With groups, I meet once a week or every other week, or sometimes even once a month. Those tools become much, much more important.

And cross-disciplinary becomes a lot more important. Because we need to have some way to come back to the conversation that we are having that we are not quite settled on yet.

Living documents become tools for communication and recording thinking. There is a distinction between recording "what is done" versus "what the group is thinking." Both are important records, but they mean different things. Doing involves actions. Thinking involves the group's thoughts about the action. Connecting what the group is thinking to what is being done is important. You can only change what you do by reflecting on the outcome. Looking at the connections between doing and thinking is powerful. The record takes on a different meaning over time and a means for shared communication across different groups.

➤ *Project meetings that focus on ideas can help the team refine and shape ideas, so it eventually develops into products or theories.*

PURPOSE SHOULD DRIVE THE AGENDA FORWARD

What is the purpose of your project meeting? What are you trying to accomplish? Why? Your purpose must define the kind of activities you engage in the meeting. Your meetings should move the agenda for innovative thinking forward. The purpose of meetings influences the kind of meeting that takes place, including frequency and logistics. Dr. Franke states that her meetings look entirely different, depending on what they were working on.

Some activities that the innovative leaders carried out to generate and refine ideas in meetings included the following: discussing readings, analyzing data, creating or examining imagery, articulating the big-picture-sharing information, and reflecting on the usefulness of tools. These activities will be described in the following sections.

Please note that even though some of the examples provided are from academia, you can adapt these ideas to fit with your team's goals regardless of discipline. Think about your long-term goals, how the project meeting fits with the larger picture. This way, the meetings are building ideas as opposed to isolated events that you check off a list.

MOVE IDEAS FORWARD THROUGH DISCUSSION

Project meetings that focus on ideas shape and refine ideas that eventually develop into products or theories. Scott Belsky (2016) point out that having a lot of brilliant ideas may not result in innovation. Therefore, approach ideas with skepticism. Ultimately, he says that action is necessary to move ideas forward and refine them.

- DISCUSS READINGS

➤ *Discussing shared readings generates ideas and increases the knowledge base.*

Reading and discussing articles enhances the team's ability to produce new thinking as well as increase the team's knowledge base. Introducing a new perspective is helpful because it creates a thinking space. As mentioned earlier, you need knowledge to be able to bend the rules to determine if something is novel or not. One form of meeting that Dr. Franke engages in with her team is reading a "common" article and discussing it.

INTERVIEW WITH DR. MEGAN FRANKE

> Sometimes it is discussion of an interesting article that might be even interesting peripherally, it is something not totally related to what we are doing, and we can look at the group and say, "let's read this and spend fifteen or twenty minutes talking about it when we see each other now.
>
> Sometimes it happens over email. Because as soon as it gets sent out, people start reading it and they start commenting on each other, so sometimes it does not last till the start of the meeting.

Reading provides a context for thinking, and even if it is not directly related to your project, it may lead to divergent thinking. You can find interesting readings or have team members share readings that relate to your project and discuss them at your meeting.

- EXAMINE DATA

  ➤ *Free-flowing examination of data allows for multiple connections and novel interpretations.*

Looking at data is another type of activity that can be done at meetings. Looking at data from the lens of "what does the data say about what is working or not working?" is helpful. As mentioned earlier, things that are not functioning can become seeds for innovation. It becomes a problem to solve. Therefore, you can ask questions such as: "What is going on?" "Why?" and "What is not working?" Dr. Cobb would ask, "What is this case of?"

Dr. Franke shared how her team looked at data. They used an organic approach so that ideas flowed freely as opposed to a predetermined structure.

INTERVIEW WITH DR. MEGAN FRANKE

> In one of our recent meeting, we were looking at some of the preschool data that we had collected and trying to make sense of why the data looks the way it does.

➤ *Having different team members come up with their own interpretation is helpful.*

So that requires lots of different people's minds that, for the task. That is different than me sitting and looking at the data on my own and saying "hmm, this is what I think."

➤ *Free flow of ideas leads to creative thought.*

Generally, the meetings are very free flowing. They are not very structured, and there is an agenda of items that we want to get to. And we start with the things that we know, that we should do that day and often we find ourselves going down some really interesting tangents.

➤ *Explore interesting tangents!*

And I often let those interesting tangents go. I don't feel that I ran these meetings. I think together I run them. I am not worried about us being "off task." I find that some of those "off task" conversations are really helpful and healthy, for the productivity of the group.

An important point Dr. Franke mentions is that the meetings are "free flowing" and not very structured. This is an important part of being able to make novel connections and not being constrained by rules or predetermined paths. The free-flowing part of a meeting allows for multiple connections to be made without constraints.

John Maxwell (2011), in his book *How Successful People Think: Change Your Thinking, Change Your Life*, points out that people need to be comfortable with uncertainty. He points out that it was important to not have a predetermined lens to look at data. Therefore, the ability to deal with uncertainty is also an important part of the creative process. Therefore, embrace uncertainty and ambiguity as part of the creative process.

Do not be discouraged by things that seem fuzzy. Realize that this is a crucial part of coming up with innovative ideas. It frees mental energy to look at things differently. At your meeting, look at data that relates to the project to identify what is happening. Be open when looking at data and not prescriptive. What does the data say? What patterns do you notice? How does it relate to the problem you are investigating?

Do you need to redefine the problem or be able to think of specific solutions? How helpful is the data? Think about what data is relevant to the problem or issue that you are trying to solve so that you are not just looking at data for the sake of looking at data.

ACTION ITEMS
Things to Consider When Examining Data

- Examine data by making sense of it as opposed to looking at it from a predefined lens.
- Consider the relevance of data to the problem. Is it useful?
- Questions to consider:
  - What does the data say?
  - What patterns do you notice?
  - How does it relate to the problem that you are investigating?
  - Do you need to redefine the problem or be able to think of specific solutions?
  - How helpful is the data?

- CREATE OR EXAMINE VISUAL IMAGERY

➤ *Visual representation of information and imagery provides STORY context for meaning making.*

Visual images, whether graphs, photographs, or videos, are powerful tools for sharing information quickly. Also, they are great conversation pieces. My graduate students usually create a graph or visual representation to capture their research findings. What we have found is that a visual can capture an event and reduce a lot of information into an image to see patterns and interactions. I have found this to be a powerful communication tool between my students and myself because we can see the big picture at an instant. This makes it easy to tweak things when you see something that seems out of sync.

INTERVIEW WITH DR. MEGAN FRANKE

I think that we share a lot of images together. Sometimes, those images are stories that carry with it. Sometimes it has particular kinds of understanding we want it to bring to the group. Sometimes images are a table format. But they tend to be things that live in a group.

So it is not every table, not every story, but there are certain stories that get taken up that get used over and over and over, and so when something comes up we can say, "Hey remember in that video, where we saw. . . . yeah, that is what we are trying to talk about right now.

➤ *Stories also provide images.*

These images that we share with each other, or stories that we tell become critical for our ongoing conversations with each other. I would say that is one thing important.

Research on creativity also points out that the ability to visualize is a vital part of the creative process. Try closing your eyes and imagine a sailboat on the ocean. Now try and visualize a storm on the ocean and the sailboat tossing around. You can imagine things without having to be at the ocean. A visual representation captures images in your mind. Sometimes it is easier to think with images.

Cyrillie Verellera and Marie-Laure Gavard-Peret (2016) presented a paper at a conference on the role of mental imagery improving user creativity. They pointed out that Einstein formulated the theory of relativity through visualization. Have people create visual representations of their thinking at the meeting, or have them bring images, graphs, charts, videos, and so on, to share with the team at the meeting.

- ARTICULATE THE BIG PICTURE

➤ *Project meetings can focus on figuring out the "big picture."*

Sometimes you may understand part of the problem. However, the "big picture" of the project might be fuzzy. A team can identify how the part fits into the "bigger picture." Dr. Nathan shared an example of how he has a sense of the pieces, but his team helped him articulate the "bigger picture" and how the pieces fit. Dr. Nathan had a large-scale project where multiple institutions collaborated. Each institution was working on a piece, so the project meetings became about articulating what these pieces were, and how they fit into the overall "big picture."

INTERVIEW WITH DR. MITCHELL NATHAN

I may go to a person and say, "How do you do this?" They may say I need to ask, "How are teacher education programs teaching pre-service teachers how to do it?" So, they might clarify and sharpen and give feedback on actual things I can observe.

One of the things that was both exciting and painful: frequently, week after week, hashing out, iterating what all these pieces were and how they all fit together. And then doing, there were parallel projects going on, but with an eye toward how they were going to get together.

The theme of hashing things out, iterating (which means revising thinking) is a painful process. Articulating the "big picture" from parts is a different perspective from how the pieces fit with the whole. Dr. Nathan pointed out that when you are sitting in a room with people with very diverse backgrounds, communication can be a challenge.

He described how he combined everyone's viewpoint into a rich integrative understanding by asking, "What is the big picture?"

INTERVIEW WITH DR. MITCHELL NATHAN

People coming from different intellectual disciplines were all sitting in a room, we talked frequently throughout the year and also once a year.

We sat in the same room and talked to one another. And had to understand one another. . . . what our contributions were and challenges were, and we could see how these things could fit together to provide this rich integrative understanding.

They all presented an enormous challenge and they were all valuable, I would say, for my own thinking and professional development. I think it leads to far greater studies.

- REFLECT ON USEFULNESS OF TOOLS

A team might be working a project, and people might not be using common tools. If this is the case, a conversation about the effectiveness of the tools can take place. Does the team agree upon a set of tools? Why or why not? Why you should use tools and which should you use are important questions to consider. Tools play an important part in how a team thinks and functions. Lave and Wenger (2002) point out that in a community of practice, people have a shared way of using tools.

- CONCRETE PROJECT METRICS ARE HELPFUL TO MONITOR PROGRESS

Having concrete things you want to produce lets you know that you are making progress and not just remaining in the idea stage. Think about what metrics you want to use to monitor your progress toward your project goal. How do you know you are being successful and moving the agenda forward?

INTERVIEW WITH DR. MITCHELL NATHAN

I think that project metric was how much research, how many publications and presentations, and also where those publications and presentations had

an impact on policy and things like that. The project was enormously influential and I think still continues to be.

This is a slightly different perspective on thinking about action items. You
know you are making progress by keeping track of the things your team
produces.

CHAPTER SUMMARY

- JOURNEY OF IDEAS TO THEORIES AND PRODUCTS REQUIRE
  ACTION

➤ *Teams can adapt and adjust action items to fit with project goals.*

You need to create conditions for ideas to develop. Ideas do not naturally
turn into innovative products or theories. Once the team generates ideas,
they must be revised and refined to develop innovative theories and
products.

As a project team leader, you must create conditions for the team to
brainstorm ideas and make novel connections by structuring project
meetings. Furthermore, you need to keep moving the agenda forward
to develop innovative theories and products by keeping track of metrics.

When you conduct project meetings, it is important to work on parts
while thinking about the big picture. This helps keep the work moving
toward innovative solutions. One of the important takeaways from this
chapter is the importance of having time to *think* and *reflect*. This is different
from just engaging in the work of "doing," such as completing the project
work. This type of thinking shifts from "What are we thinking?" as a group
to "What are we doing?" Ideally, it helps to think about the relationship
between doing and thinking. This helps you come up with new insights.

When a team gets together to think, it is important that everyone is on
the same page. When the team frequently meets, then a shared understanding, language, and tools develop. However, when the meetings are
more sporadic, or only part of the team can meet, it is important when the
team meets to understand each other's perspective before providing input.

This chapter presents the Three Levels of Sense-Making Framework
that can be used in project meetings. The first level of sense-making is to
ensure that everyone shares their perspective, and the team listens and
asks questions. The second level of sense-making involves examining
commonalities and differences between one another's perspective and
brainstorming ideas. The third level of sense-making involves explicitly
recording new insights and connecting them to the "big picture" and

coming up with action items to move the agenda forward. The purpose should drive project meetings. A variety of techniques such as discussing readings, analyzing data, creating or examining imagery, articulating the big picture, sharing information, and reflecting on the usefulness of tools can be used to move the project agenda forward.

STRATEGIES FOR MOVING THE AGENDA FORWARD

- Identify the problem that your team is trying to solve.
- Make a list of goals that you want to accomplish in the project. Establish metrics so that you know that you are making progress. (Be specific, such as the number of research articles, or products, etc.)
- Break down goals into manageable chunks.
- Create a timeline, and map out what needs to be accomplished and when. This will help you plan your time.
- Create a calendar with your team. Decide when it makes sense to meet and in what format. Figure out the purpose for your meetings so that people know it ahead of time. Make sure these plans are flexible and adaptable as things come up.
- Facilitate project meetings to move thinking forward.

QUESTIONS TO ADAPT TO PUSH THINKING TO THE NEXT LEVEL
(Questions adapted from Lamberg [2012].)

Questions to push and challenge thinking:

- What do you mean by that?
- Does everyone understand what _____ is saying?
- Can you explain _____ part?
- What are you thinking and why?

Questions to analyze each other's thinking:

- What is similar about these explanations?
- What differences do you notice?
- What patterns do you see?

Questions to extend thinking:

- What are your thoughts about what we discussed?
- How does this address the problem or issue being discussed?
- What are the big ideas here that we need to pay attention to?
- How do these ideas help us reach our goal?

Questions to synthesize thinking:

- What have we agreed upon? Are we on the same page?
- What problems do we need to address? Why?
- What are the new insights that we have learned?

Questions to move the agenda forward:

- What are our next steps?
- What are you planning on working on and bringing to the next meeting?
- What resources do we need?
- What issues or concerns do you have?
- Where we are now, and how does this fit with the big picture?

Lamberg, Teruni, *Whole Class Mathematics Discussions: Improving In-Depth Mathematical Thinking and Learning,* first edition, © 2013. Reprinted by permission of Pearson Education, Inc., New York, New York.

ACTION ITEMS THAT YOU CAN ADAPT TO PLAN A MEETING

- Determine your focus agenda for the meeting; what do you want to accomplish (goals)?
- Notify team members of what they need to prepare for the meeting (a slide, a handout, answers to questions, reports, etc.).
- Start the meeting by stating the goals you want to accomplish in the meeting and connect to the big picture.
- Discuss the problem or issue you are working on.
- Have the team share, although perhaps not everyone needs to share what they are thinking or working on, or any information relevant to solving the problem or issue that is the focus of the meeting. The goal is to find the "common ground." Encourage others to listen to others' perspectives and ask clarifying questions.
- Discuss what they notice that is similar or different or other ideas they are thinking about as they listen to others' explanations.
- Summarize in a document and record key ideas that emerge.
- Identify "next steps."
- Connect to the big-picture goal to see how the team is making progress.
- Use an iterative design approach; figure out what is working and what is not and try things out and refine thinking over time. Think about the meeting as part of the journey of building ideas, as opposed to a single, isolated event.

3

How to Consider End Users' Needs When Testing and Refining Design

Nobody cares how much you know, until they know how much you care.

—Theodore Roosevelt

Why do we innovate? We innovate because we want to solve a problem and make something better, faster, or cheaper. Ultimately, we need to think about the people we are trying to help. Innovation is useful only if it addresses a real need. Therefore, thinking about the context of how the innovation will be used is helpful.

For example, a state-of-the-art computer screen for the public that costs $100,000 does not make sense. Even if the screen is mind-blowing and innovative, many will not be able to afford it. The high cost will prevent many people from purchasing it. Dr. Gary Pisano (2015) wrote an article that was published in the *Harvard Business Review* titled "You Need an Innovation Strategy."

In this article, he explains the importance of an innovation creating value for customers. Dr. Pisano points out that the innovation must provide value for the customer, such as saving money. The innovation must benefit society, such as in improved health and clean water. He points out that making life easier and better for others creates value. It involves making a product better, cheaper, or more reliable. He writes that choosing the kind of value the innovation will create, and building on that, is an important part of the design process.

Therefore, consider the situation from a holistic perspective when innovating. This means you must pay careful attention to the customer and the end user of your innovation. One way to think about innovating is that it is for the betterment of society.

> ➤ *When designing an innovation, ask how it can help the people it serves.*

The end user is the person who ends up using the innovation. The customer is the person who purchased the product out of some need. Both needs must be considered for the innovation to be used and serve a need.

INTERVIEW WITH DR. KAMIL A. JBEILY

> All innovations must serve a purpose and address a need. Why we did what we did in Texas Regional Collaboratives was because there was a *need*. They changed the curriculum, they changed the assessments, they changed the text book. . . . You innovate by asking yourself, "How can I be of better service to the people that I am serving now or those that I have not served yet?"

A real need in the community is a reason to innovate, as shared by Dr. Jbeily, the founder and former director of Texas Regional Collaboratives at the University of Texas at Austin. In education, the end user might be the student using a new tool or technique to learn. Perhaps it is a teacher trying out a new lesson or a teaching method, such as whole-class discussions. It may be a school that is implementing a new reading program. Perhaps the end user is the district that is implementing a new curriculum. It may be a state or even a nation that is developing new standards and rolling them out for implementation.

The size of the community served can be small or large, depending on the context of the innovation. Testing and refining an innovation in the field is helpful. For example, design research has been used in education and other fields, such as engineering, to test innovations in different contexts. This is when an innovation is tested and refined in a context based on how the users respond.

Following are some of the ways the user's point of view has been considered in the field of education. These include teacher action research, lesson study, and design research.[1] Teacher action research is one way to test and refine an innovation in education settings. This is when a teacher tries out an intervention and then collects data to see how the intervention is working and adjusts teaching based on student learning.

Other techniques, such as lesson study, can be used to improve teaching. This is where a team of teachers plans lessons together, one person teaches the lesson, everyone observes and provides feedback. The group debriefs afterward to figure out what worked and what didn't and how the lesson can be improved. This is not an exhaustive list of how to test innovations in an education setting. The main point is that there are different approaches for testing and refining an innovation within a field as opposed to prescribing a solution.

INSIDER VIEW PROVIDES REALISTIC PERSPECTIVE

An important part of innovating involves understanding the world through the lens of the community you are serving. This is different from simply being an observer or studying a topic from an academic point of view. Innovating so that it solves real problems is much easier if using an insider perspective. Dr. Gutiérrez, a professor at the University of Illinois at Urbana-Champaign, explains that her own lived, real-world experiences and those of others on her team provide valuable insight to innovate. The combination of knowledge and experience is powerful.

➤ *An organic approach to innovating supports creative solutions.*

Dr. Gutiérrez describes the creative process as an organic endeavor. Her goal is to support teachers to be advocates for children from a social-justice point of view.

INTERVIEW WITH DR. ROCHELLE GUTIÉRREZ

A lot of my work is very organic. I try to be responsive to the situation and to the people in it. I don't start out thinking that I know exactly what I am going to do. I have a direction but not a destination. I know that right now that I am going north. I don't have a specific address that I am trying to get to. I know that right now that that is where I want to go.

When this project started, I knew that there was not a lot written out there about the politics that mathematics teachers face in schools or the forms of knowledge that would be useful for them in navigating those politics. But I have quotes from teachers that I have studied from my own experience; I have learned from people who are doing it.

Some of the work that I learned, I had learned in a community activist perspective that was not always applied to teaching. I had experiences as an activist and I knew that teachers were not always prepared to be activists. But, there were a lot of overlapping skills and sensitivities that being an activist offers to teaching. I had to be responsible to the teachers that I was preparing.

I had to be responsible and not act as if I didn't see the politics they were facing, because that wasn't part of "mathematics," or that I didn't have tools that worked for me that I could share. So, even if the field of mathematics education didn't recognize this political knowledge as important for mathematics teachers to develop, I still had to do the right thing and respond to their needs. It became a part of how I do teacher education.

An organic approach as opposed to following a prescribed path provides opportunities for innovation. She shared how she developed tools to support teachers with social justice issues. She gave some examples of the context that influenced the development of tools.

Interview with Dr. Rochelle Gutiérrez

The tools came out of iterations. Back in 2006, I started doing something I call "In My Shoes." It addresses political scenarios that teachers face. It's one way I support teachers to practice responding to the politics in their schools. For example, a teacher starts out saying "This thing happened to me today. I was in the hallway, and there was another teacher who told me that I couldn't let Geraldo do this worksheet because he did not have an excuse for being late; that is how 'those kids' are." So, in this scenario, the teacher didn't know what to do when the other teacher told her that she couldn't let Geraldo do the worksheet. She knew she wanted to let him do it and that it was the right thing to do. But, this other teacher, maybe a veteran teacher or someone who holds authority over her, is telling her she can't.

So, what is this teacher in the scenario supposed to do? Early on in my teaching, I'd just have teachers give each other advice. Then, over the years, we realized that they really needed to practice standing up for themselves and their students. So now, we don't just develop strategies in a group for how a teacher might respond, we actually role-play it.

We have the teacher who faced the scenario practice either convincing this person why she should allow the student to do the worksheet and how all students should have opportunities to do mathematical work. Or, maybe the strategy is to just nod her head politely and walk around this person and find another teacher who would be her ally and help support her to advocate for Geraldo and other students like him. There are a bunch of strategies we have developed for doing this kind of work that has come out of watching teachers navigate their politics over so many years.

So, there are all kinds of scenarios that teachers face on an everyday basis that get in the way of how they truly want to teach, of teaching high quality and meaningful mathematics to students. You might have a scenario where a teacher says, "My principal was explaining the achievement gap and said to us that it is due to 'black culture,' and 'they are disengaging each other from school.'

So, in my role as a teacher educator, I'm thinking, "How do we help the teacher convey something to the principal like, 'So, you are saying that black culture is the one thing preventing us from closing the achievement gap?'" But, she has to say it without getting him mad at her or getting fired.

She shared another example. One of her students observed a classroom where a teacher had a group of students in the back of the classroom that she ignored. The teacher's attitude was "If they don't bug me, I don't bug them." These types of scenarios led Dr. Gutiérrez and her team to develop a protocol around "In My Shoes." This tool was intended for teachers to be advocates for their students and learn how to problem solve situations related to political and social-justice issues. Now, several teacher educators across the nation use a version of "In My Shoes" in their teacher-education programs.

INNOVATE LIKE A JAZZ
GROUP THROUGH RIGOROUS IMPROVISATION

Creatively combining ideas by drawing from real-world lived experiences and knowledge is an important part of innovating. Dr. Gutiérrez approached this perspective like a jazz band creating music. She explains that her team had not just academic knowledge, but knowledge of lived experiences of marginalized students. That is, her team of doctoral students were black and Chicanx.

That allowed them to create and brainstorm in ways that related directly to the historically marginalized students they were trying to help teachers serve better. She emphasized that the purpose needs to be determined. However, the process of innovating to meet one's needs should be flexible and adaptable.

INTERVIEW WITH DR. ROCHELLE GUTIÉRREZ

So, in some ways creating my team and working as a team, we call it rigorous improvisation. Because it is just like how a jazz group would be. You don't know the thing that you are going to produce. You are going to start, and everyone clearly has skills, and someone is like "oh she is playing that note, I am going to add this thing to it."

The process that Dr. Gutiérrez describes is the process of brainstorming and generating ideas as a group. This process involved building on each other's thinking spontaneously without a predetermined agenda. Innovating this way allows for ideas to flow and connect freely.

Interview with Dr. Rochelle Gutiérrez

So much of the professional development that we did with the teachers . . .

We did not have it scripted to say, "First we are going to do this, and then we are going to do this and then we are going to test to see if they got it." Instead, we looked at "What do they need right now?" and "How are we going to respond?"

The process described involves being adaptive to the needs of the community she was serving. The questions that she asked were an important part of focusing the direction of brainstorming. An important part of innovating is to create, adapt, and improvise while keeping in mind the community you are serving. This process also involves asking the right questions because these questions will drive decision making. Consider what questions you are trying to address. This is different from having questions with right or wrong answers.

Interview with Dr. Rochelle Gutiérrez

We don't have an endpoint. . . . It was more like "what meaning are they making in the model of teacher education, and what meaning are they making in activities like "In My Shoes?" So, what we created was accomplished because no single person was positioned as the expert. We had knowledge outside of the university that was brought in. . . .

Creative ideas are much more likely to happen when an organic approach to brainstorming is used. Therefore, be open and flexible when brainstorming. Another part is to value everyone's ideas as being equally important as opposed to a hierarchy of ideas.

➢ *Consider the usefulness of the innovation from the user's point of view.*

The design process must consider the users' perception of innovation. Dr. Clayton Christensen (2013), who wrote *The Innovators' Dilemma*, points out that when innovating, disruptive technologies such as smart phones, change the way that people typically do things. Therefore, plans for supporting user *learning* must be considered in the design and implementation process.

INTERVIEW WITH DR. PRIYAN FERNANDO

> ➤ *Simplicity is key in innovating and meeting end user/customer needs.*

Most people lack the patience to take time to figure things out when having to try or use something new. Mr. Priyan Fernando, chairman of Brandix Lanka Limited, shared his thoughts about innovation. Over the years he has held many influential leadership positions that have made an international impact. As a senior advisor to the Boston Consulting Group, he is known to be an innovative leader in the business world. When interviewed, he shared the key to innovating: *SIMPLICITY.*

He gave the example of a cell phone. People like the obvious simplicity of having many things in one device. Thus, most innovation has happened around the support of that device. He pointed out that when you look at things from the customer-needs point of view, it is easier to examine what would really resonate. He said that problem solving around the customers' needs is a "great unifier."

> ➤ *Institutional support is needed to change the culture to innovate.*

Mr. Fernando points out that companies must look at themselves differently. This means that they should look at the company outside-in through the lens of the customer. This horizontal view cuts across the silos of the enterprise and follows how work gets done. He called this a "panoramic view." These conditions are critical as teams collaborate across organizational silos to innovate. Innovation must be rewarded and supported within an institution. "When changing the culture, one must focus on defining it, providing resources to enable it and finally changing the performance reward mechanism to reinforce it. If there are no consequences, you will be reinforcing the status quo."[2]

Consider what you are trying to accomplish, and the structures in place that can afford and constrain innovation within your current institution. What are some things that are helpful in your current setting to innovate? What must change? Dr. Jbeily (n.d.) wrote the following in *Transforming the Culture of Education in the United States Our Future Depends on It*:

> Barriers and Stumbling blocks must be viewed as challenges and carefully managed with strong determination and commitment to transforming them into stepping stones. Barriers include: discomfort with change, reluctance to collaborate due to the momentum of old paradigms of individualistic initiative and competition.

➤ *When designing, look at things from an interdisciplinary lens.*

Looking at things from an interdisciplinary perspective is helpful. Dr. Howard Gardner, author of *Five Minds for the Future*, identified a disciplined mind as one of the five minds for the future in his framework. A person with a disciplined mind has a deep understanding of a discipline and can grasp concepts from other disciplines and see connections.

What Dr. Gardner means is that analyzing situations from an interdisciplinary perspective is powerful. He points out that synthesizing knowledge and information, in addition to seeing connections among disciplines, is an important skill. This is like Mr. Fernando's recommendation of having a panoramic view of processes. Dr. Gardner points out that people should be able to use information in new and novel ways. The ability to think about information in new and unique ways is an important part of innovation.

Looking at situations from a holistic perspective helps. Dr. Nathan shared that when he started his career, he was interested in artificial intelligence and robotics. He was intrigued by how robotics could move the manufacturing field forward. However, he realized that thinking about how humans interact with machines is important to make smart people, not just smart machines. So, he thought about what the field of psychology could offer. He explained that today, we are at a point where self-driving cars are being invented. He noted that practical solutions are not enough. Rather, looking at things from a real-world-application perspective is needed.

➤ *Look at practicality of solutions from a real-world perspective.*

INTERVIEW WITH DR. MITCHELL NATHAN

> Engineers might find practical solutions for them, but they don't necessarily do it alone. And they could do it in an informed approach from other fields. If you know something about computer science and engineers, you know that they solve problems that have a technical elegance. But that may not in any way resemble the nature of the actual problem from the outside world. They may solve it so that it may match the technology.

Dr. Nathan points out that it was important to think about the practicality of solutions from a real-world perspective of the user. This means you need to think about the end user from a holistic viewpoint. Just focusing on the technical aspects and ignoring the people part is not helpful. These aspects include what problem the innovation will address.

> ➤ *Feedback from the community is important to develop innovation through testing and revising.*

Testing an innovation based on feedback from end users is an important part of the design process. Making a difference requires paying attention to feedback and use from end users.

It is one thing to learn how to swim by reading a book. However, it is only when you get in the water and experience what it is really like that your perspective changes.

Try swimming in an ocean or river; it is a very different experience from swimming in a pool. You learn nuances by doing and experiencing. Getting feedback from people is very helpful to get a sense of real-world situations and to innovate in a way that is meaningful. Understanding the problem situations in the community is just as important for coming up with a solution.

INNOVATION SHOULD REFLECT AN INTERPLAY BETWEEN THE DESIGNERS AND END USERS

Elisa Giaccardi and Gerhard Fisher (2008), authors of the article, "Creativity and Evaluation: A Metadesign Perspective," caution innovators not to just rely on the End Users' definition of the problem as well. The problem may be ill defined. Also, the world is ever changing. When you get feedback to design an intervention or innovative solution, the context in which it might be used might change.

Therefore, this is something you must keep in mind as your team innovates. Giaccardi and Fisher recommend participatory design approaches with the end users so that you can get feedback along the way as opposed to doing it at the beginning and end. The goal is not just to get reactive feedback but have the end user participate along with the way of the design.

Dr. Franke had an intriguing view of her role as an innovative leader. She believes that understanding and extending the use of innovation is also a role of a leader. She observed how teachers used the ideas from the Cognitively Guided Instruction (CGI) project to support student learning. She discovered that teachers were using the ideas in innovative ways the designers had not anticipated. By observing how the ideas of children's thinking were being used in the field, she reflected on what she saw. The "aha moment" was when she noticed how the teachers were innovatively using the tools. She could recognize the innovation and build on their thinking and extend it.

INTERVIEW WITH DR. MEGAN FRANKE

> Helping other people see that and why I think that is so important and in-
> teresting!
> Sometimes other people do, it is up to me to notice where the things are
> emerging, and figure out how to raise them up a little bit.

This view has been helpful for the advancement of the CGI project. Many
projects might have ideas that fizzle out quickly. What is unique about
this project is that the work has been sustained, developed, and refined
over the past thirty years!

You may find that different types of users need varying levels of support.
Some might need precise directions; others might need coaching. You need
to tailor the end user support based on the needs of the end user.

CONSIDER THE CONTEXT FOR INNOVATION

> ➤ *Pay attention to the larger context of the end user.*

Think about the community you are serving and the environment in
which the innovation will be used. Dr. Cobb points out how important
it is to be proactive in getting feedback and understanding the context in
which you work. When he first started doing research in the classroom,
he said that his team's focus was helping students and teachers. They did
not consider things happening outside the classroom. This would be the
natural thing to do.

You want to help kids learn, so you are going to figure out the best
way to help kids learn. You are going to put all your energy into coming
up with the best solution. He learned the hard way that you need to pay
attention to the larger context in which you innovate. He had not anticipated the roadblocks that were going to be set by the school board. They
did not give teachers the flexibility to adapt the district curricula they
were using and trying new things.

Even though they had come up with some innovative, cutting-edge
ideas, teachers experienced resistance from implementing them. He
learned a valuable lesson about paying attention to stakeholders and the
need to take the context into account.

INTERVIEW WITH DR. PAUL COBB

> The first large project that I directed, . . . we ended up with working with
> quite a few teachers. Some experiences there really stuck with me. There

was a new school board, a very conservative school board who wanted to control the math curriculum. Our project became a center of the dispute, the school board on the one hand and the teachers and principals ended up supporting it.

Teachers who are involved in the work have become quite committed to it, and this went on for two years. I did not see any of this coming because we were just focusing on what was going on in the classroom. I almost did not anticipate this. A lot of sleepless nights, in the end, the teachers took over the leadership of the group, and we consulted with them and provided them with information.

A colleague studied this and wrote a chapter about it. And the teachers won out in the end. But I swore after that I would never do teacher development work or project again unless I had a way of understanding school and district context. *Not reactive, but I could be proactive.*

Think about the project you are working on. You are trying to come up with an idea to make life better for others. You are probably working on a great solution. You also need to consider the context where you will be able to implement the innovation.

Think About . . .

- *What are some hidden forces and things that you need to think about?*
- *What can you do to be proactive so that the intervention is successfully implemented or used?*

The question is: Do you give up trying? Or try anyway and think about working with the larger context and find ways to communicate?

We have an incredible opportunity to learn from Dr. Cobb's experience. We get to learn about his next project where he paid attention to the institutional context of the school district. He used his learning experience from his previous project to change the way he worked the next time. This experience is an important part of innovating.

Building on experiences and knowledge is helpful. In the next project, Dr. Cobb considered the institutional context and studied how that affected how he worked with the teachers.

INTERVIEW WITH DR. PAUL COBB

> It was over that course of that project that we found that looking at school and district context was far more helpful than I had anticipated. It was just not about being proactive. It also had explanatory power.

Understanding how the school district culture impacted his work was valuable for working with teachers as well as rethinking approaches and interventions. Dr. Cobb shared how he went on to develop a larger scale project where they developed tools to help districts improve their math instruction. After that, his next project involved developing tools for teachers.

INTERVIEW WITH DR. PAUL COBB

> The MIST project was about developing a *theory of action*. We found that districts struggled with the implementation. The form happened, not the function. The school leaders spent time in classrooms and gave feedback.

> The next step is to support districts in implementation processes. The first step was developing practical measures.

> ➤ *Each step of the design process, step back and think about the direction that you are going in to ensure you are meeting needs of the community you are serving.*

A great insight that Dr. Cobb shared was that when you innovate at each step you need to step back and think about the direction that you are going in. You need to be flexible and adapt the innovation to address the needs of the community that you are serving

ACTION ITEMS

> ➤ Think about the *user* of the innovation from a holistic perspective.
> ➤ Think about the larger context in which you innovate. Are there hidden forces that might constrain the implementation of the innovation? How can you address them?
> ➤ How do you plan to get participatory feedback from the end user?

LEVERAGE INTELLECTUAL AND MATERIAL RESOURCES

Most projects need material and human resources. Finding creative ways to maximize human and material resources can enhance the success of a project.

CASE STUDY: NEVADA MATHEMATICS PROJECT

> For example, in the Nevada Mathematics Project, we had a budget that was funded for certain kinds of things. Therefore, by combining the work of multiple projects such as Dr. Nathan's project on gestures and Dr. Chang's work on nanotechnology, we could innovate and provide a higher quality project because of this collaboration. We could leverage space from the school districts to host the sessions and work with the district leaders to recruit teachers and communicate with others.

What human resources and material resources are available for your project? Can you think of creative ways to leverage human and material resources to make your project a success?

Think About . . .

- *What resources do you need to complete the project?*
- *What resources can you creatively leverage to enhance your project?*
- *What resources do your project team members have access to?*
- *Are stakeholders willing to contribute resources for the service you are providing?*

➤ *Identify key agents within the system to get things done.*

Getting things done can be a challenge if you must do everything yourself. This is particularly the case if you are working across organizational units and across different communities. Identifying key players and having them as part of your team is helpful.

CASE STUDY: NEVADA MATHEMATICS PROJECT

> It would have been difficult to recruit teachers from across the state in every single school district if I had had to contact each teacher

individually. However, the district leaders had access to an internal communication system to get the word out. This made it easier to get things done. Key contributors play an important role as "brokers" within your project as well as across organizational communities.

Think About . . .

- *What are your project needs?*
- *Who are the key agents on your team or stakeholders who can help with the flow of the work?*

REALIZE THAT THE END USER DECIDES HOW TO USE INNOVATION AND SCALE-UP

How an innovation gets used might be different from what the innovator intended. Therefore, thinking about how it could be used is important. If the innovation is very prescriptive, chances are it may not be used exactly as designed. This is an interesting perspective to think about. How do you scale-up the innovation? How do you allow it to spread to the end user when your team is not specifically available to give specific directions or demonstrate how to use it?

The bottom line is you can't control the end user; rather you can try to understand from their perspective how the innovation can be used. You can adjust the design. Also, you can have an open mind to the possibilities of use that you may not have thought about.

Dr. Franke has an interesting perspective on innovation and how it is used in the community. The CGI project has been around for more than thirty years. This is an opportunity to see the mature state of an innovative project that has evolved. It was important to Dr. Franke that the teachers owned the innovation and adapted it. She pointed out that she did not want to control it as the "right way to do it." When they first started, they were prescriptive.

INTERVIEW WITH DR. MEGAN FRANKE

In the initial experimental study, we had thought we would give teachers example lessons and units that they could take and use in their classrooms. It was an initial proposal because it was too hard to tell teachers to figure this out all on their own. You must give them some materials that they could use in their classroom. When I started to develop some materials, it started to be really hard to do because it is not about the materials, right? So, having all the stuff built into the materials started to be really complicated.

THE SCALE-UP OF INNOVATION FROM THE
COGNITIVELY GUIDED INSTRUCTION PROJECT

Dr. Franke discovered that some end users used the innovation differently than anticipated by the designers. She was intrigued by what happened. This means that you need to have an open lens when looking at how the innovation is used.

People's backgrounds and experiences influence how innovation is perceived and used. The innovators can look at the end users' use of the innovations as to whether they used it correctly or incorrectly. Another perspective is to pay attention to the end user; the innovators discovered new possibilities that moved their thinking forward.

INTERVIEW WITH DR. MEGAN FRANKE

> You create this awesome learning opportunity where we had the opportunity to learn from really thoughtful smart teachers. So, we did not really choose to do it the same way.

Dr. Franke explained that the teachers drove their agenda of innovation as illustrated in figure 3.1. Once they had finished their experimental study, the students were learning at a sophisticated pace. This created a situation where the teachers did not know where to go next with their lessons to support their students. They asked her team for help.

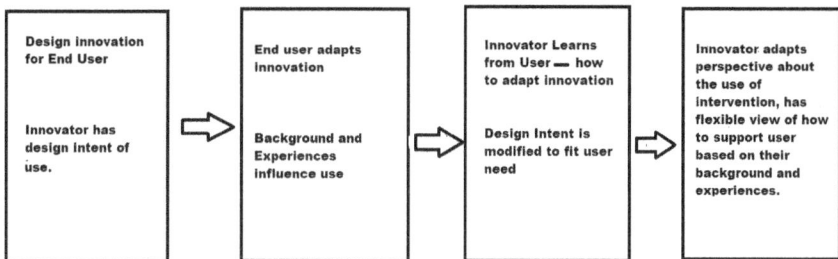

Figure 3.1.   Dr. Franke's Perspective of the Journey of the Cognitively Guided Instruction Project
Teruni Lamberg

INTERVIEW WITH DR. MEGAN FRANKE

> "You have to help us figure out what to do." *I don't think that would have happened if we had not made that initial shift in providing teachers that kind of power.*

Generativity is an important part of spreading the innovation. The reality is that you can't control how the innovation gets used. Also, your team cannot train everyone on how to use the innovation. End users learn from each other as well. This is an important part of spreading or scaling-up the innovation. This is something you should think about when considering how your innovation will be used.

> Here is the interplay from research. It started out as "let's help them use this knowledge." We very quickly found out that we did not know what teachers know and that is not our expertise. Our job became to learn from teachers on what they could do to innovate and to raise that up. Help other people learn from that and for us to learn from them the ways to extend CGI.
>
> This idea of GENERATIVITY is a really important part of our work. The notion that we all have to have knowledge about children's thinking. The more we learn, the more our knowledge evolves. Different people because of their experience are going to get different kinds of knowledge, get information, get different ideas and have that on the table. People are going to learn from each other and extend it.

Dr. Franke's biggest insight is that you can't control how people use the innovation because individuals have different experiences and knowledge that influence how they adapt an innovation. Her biggest insight was that it was important to let go of control.

> It was not our initial idea, but it quickly became the approach that we took in CGI. And to really step back and our wanting to control it. It emerges over and over in our work that people want us to control it! I want as a leader to let it go! We are all thinking about it together. In ways that advance the work.

Dr. Franke learned that by being open, teachers came up with some innovative ways to use CGI, and she was intrigued by that. She felt that the work belonged to the community to innovate and has taken on a different life of its own. The organic nature of how the innovation gets used and adapted in the community involves finding people to use the innovation in new ways and learn from the process.

> So that my job as the leader in CGI is to look out for people who are putting ideas about how to extend CGI in interesting ways. I can highlight and connect to other people, who would benefit from having conversations with

them and also move the work forward. So, instead of thinking about controlling it, I am trying to think about how to grow it.

> ➤ *Interplay between innovation and end users involves adaptability.*

What was interesting about Dr. Franke's perspective is that the group observed how the innovation was used in the community. They learned how to adapt it and extend it from fresh perspectives. This is a different perspective from being prescriptive about how to use it. Dr. Franke feels that people can learn from each other and can learn ways of how to make the innovation different, better, and more useful.

CASE STUDY: NEVADA MATHEMATICS PROJECT

We used the tools and the knowledge developed by the CGI project in our work in the Nevada Mathematics Project. As I reflected on what we did, I had to admit that we adapted the tools to fit the needs of our teachers. I infused it with my work, the framework from my book *Whole Class Mathematical Discussions* (2012).

Therefore, we adapted and extended the innovation and built on it based on what the CGI project had done. If we had used it in a prescribed way, we might not have been as effective with its use because we would not have adapted to the end user, the teacher, but also, we were influenced by our understanding and background knowledge to use the tools.

The question becomes "If the innovation takes on a life of its own by the end users, then what must we pay attention to when innovating?" Giaccardi and Fisher (2008) point out that a co-adaptive process between users and a system must be developed. They explain that users could pinpoint breakdowns and opportunities. It is this insight that can lead to new understandings and knowledge.

SOMETIMES INNOVATIONS ARE HIT OR MISS: YOU WON'T KNOW THAT UNTIL YOU TRY!

The important part of innovating is that you make the best judgment to serve the end user. Sometimes you might find that you were right on track and other times, you might be back to the drawing board. Either way, you won't know until you try things and get feedback from the end user. Getting as much input at the beginning and during the design process, and studying the innovation that gets used is helpful. Sometimes the end user might ask for help or even come up with suggestions. In this case, the end users might drive innovation out of a need. If your team is sensitive to addressing a need, this becomes an excellent opportunity to innovate.

INTERVIEW WITH DR. MEGAN FRANKE

> And honestly, is this a place where I think the work we do further addresses the marginalized status on the community and push back? The part of it that is ORGANIC. Once you start doing that. People come to you with opportunities and ideas and sometimes you don't have time to think about something you should do or not.

> *You do it because you want to support the people and you do it because it is something good for the community. There has been stuff that I have done that has been long-term innovative sustaining things. There have been things that I have done that I think, gee whiz, why did I do that and I wish I had done that differently. Sometimes the organic stuff can be a hit or miss in terms of long-term sustaining innovation.*

> Those organic things, but those organic things are driven by the needs of the community so, those are the things that I feel most compelled to take up, and that is where I think a lot of innovation happens. Because of a feeling that they need to do something. And they are in a situation where they want to do something.

The key part is building a relationship between stakeholders whom you are innovating for. This creates a communication feedback loop that is important to build high-quality innovations that make an impact. This is a critical piece of the work that Dr. Franke and her team were doing. They were listening, adapting, and responding. If you take this part of your work out, you miss an important opportunity to address real needs. In academia, this might be considered ivory tower academics that are not grounded in the reality of the real world.

Think about your project. What is your innovation? How is the user using the innovation? Pay attention! Are there some ways that it is being used that you can build on? How can you support people with varying levels of knowledge? It is critical to understand the use of the innovation from their lens or perspective. Also, recognize ways the innovation can be adapted and used that you might not have thought of. Therefore, how can you capitalize the new perspectives and support the spread of the innovation?

CHAPTER SUMMARY

Engage in Provocative Thinking

> ➤ *Opportunity to leverage resources and creatively problem solve for innovation.*

Engaging in provocative thinking involves considering the community that is being served and making sure if a real-need is addressed. This process involves making things better, faster, or cheaper. In other words, the innovation must benefit society.

The innovation can be designed by a team to make a profound influence. It may also involve doing something at a microlevel that makes a difference or at a larger scale. The scale does not matter; the process is the same. The bottom line is that innovating involves learning from the process, designing, and adapting things to help the community you serve.

This process involves considering customer/end user's perspective in the design process. Think about the problem from the standpoint of the end user and design an intervention that addresses a need. Simplicity is the key to a successful innovation. Figure out ways to harness material and human resources and get feedback. Designs should be tested and refined in the field for optimal usefulness.

You must consider not only the innovation, but also the conditions in which it would be used. There might be hidden forces that you may not have thought about. These hidden forces might involve how people typically do things, and they may require a change. Also, think about supports in your organization or community that are needed to implement the innovation.

Scaling up innovation may take on a life of its own. Don't be constrained in trying to control the innovation. Rather, figure out ways to support the spread of innovation through constructive ways.

STRATEGIES FOR THINKING
ABOUT THE END USER AND REFINING DESIGN

- Simplicity is key in innovating and meeting customer needs. Strive for simplicity when being innovative. People like things more efficient, faster, and/or better.
- Does innovation address real-world needs of the customer and end user
  - Who is your customer/end user?
  - What are the characteristics of end users?

- ○ What are their needs? How are the needs currently addressed? What works and what does not?
- ○ How might the innovation be used? What is the context?
- ○ What are their perceptions, thoughts, and feelings about the innovation?
- ○ What kind of supports does the end user need?
- Plan of action for feedback from the end user/customer before, during, and after is needed.
- The innovation from your end user? Plan: consider when, where, and how to get feedback from the end user/customer. Also consider what kind of feedback is needed during the design process.
  - ○ What is the end user's perception of the problem?
  - ○ What kind of solution is the end user requesting?
  - ○ What are some of the current solutions, and what works and what does not work?
  - ○ Make a list of ways you are going to get feedback on the innovation. (For example, be specific, such as you are going to use focus groups, observations, surveys.)
  - ○ How are you going to use this information to improve design decisions? At what meetings would this be taken into account?
- Consider the larger context of end user. Even if the solution is innovative, what is the context in which the innovation will be used? What might be possible barriers in the implementation of the innovation? Think about how to address these barriers.
- Evaluate and act in each step of the design process. Step back and think about the direction that you are going to ensure you are meeting the needs of the customer and end user.
- Leverage intellectual and material resources *from* your team and stakeholders. Draw upon experiences and knowledge from the team in the design process.
  - ○ What resources does your project team have access to?
  - ○ Are stakeholders willing to contribute resources for the service you are providing?
- Identify key agents within the system to get things done. These may be individuals who have access to the end users or are able to communicate information to stakeholders. They play a valuable role in the success of a project. This is because information can be shared easily with stakeholders as well as getting general feedback on the design or implementation of the innovation.
- Consider the scale-up of innovation. How might it be used in a different context, and what kind of supports might be needed for the success of implementation.

Think About . . .
Who is your end user?

- *Create a sketch and make a list of the characteristics of the customer/ end user.*
- *What problem are you trying to solve?*
- *Think about the problem that will be solved and the context in which the innovation will be used.*
- *Make a list of characteristics of the problem and the context in which the innovation will be used.*

What is the end users' perceived usefulness of the innovation?

- *Try to understand how the end user might perceive the usefulness of the innovation. Anticipate how the actual innovation might be used within a context.*
- *Get feedback from the end user during the design process not just at the end. Adapt design based on feedback. This will help the team refine innovation according to real needs as opposed to perceived needs. If the End User does not perceive it to be useful or fill a need, then the chances are the innovation will not be used.*

NOTES

1. Design research is a research methodology where an intervention is designed, implemented and improved by trying it out in the field. Researchers systematically study the design process and document the design decisions made. See the following article for more information about design research: T. D. Lamberg and J. A. Middleton (2009). "Design Research Perspectives Transitioning from Individual Microgenetic Interviews to a Whole-Class Teaching Experiment." Educational Researcher, 38(4), 233–245. http://dx.doi.org/10.3102/0013189X09334206.

2. Interview with Mr. Priyan Fernando conducted by Teruni Lamberg.

4

How to Communicate Effectively with Teams and Stakeholders

Get rid of corporate speak and speak from the heart. Whatever you say is taken at face value. The ability to share thoughts without fear of consequences is what creates a fertile ground for innovation. Build on a thought; it can snowball into something worthwhile.

—Priyan Fernando, senior advisor to Boston Consulting group, chairman of Brandix Lanka, Limited

The flow of ideas, information, and knowledge among and within the team and stakeholders allows for innovation to happen. This process is like lighting a light bulb with a battery and wires. The electricity must pass through the wires to make the light bulb turn on. Similarly, the flow of ideas, information, and knowledge is like the electricity going through the wires.

Communication is needed to generate ideas, innovate, and accomplish great things. Salma Alguezaui and Raffaele Filieri wrote an article titled "Investigating the Role of Social Capital in Innovation: Sparse versus Dense Network." They point out that managing knowledge is something that people should strategically consider. This means you need to come up with a plan on how to ensure that relevant, timely, and effective communication takes place.

There are two kinds of knowledge. Alguezaui and Filieri describe the difference between *explicit* and *tacit* knowledge. Explicit knowledge is made up of facts, and it is easier to pass along. However, tacit knowledge is much harder to share. Alguezaui and Filieri point out tacit knowledge is made up of relevant, actionable, information that is partially based on information (Davenport and Prusak 1998, 5). They point out that tacit knowledge is essential for innovation.

CASE STUDY: NEVADA MATHEMATICS PROJECT

We experienced the difference between these two types of knowledge as a project team. For example, when the Nevada Mathematics

Project team initially met, we had shared explicit knowledge about the tasks that we were planning on doing with teachers. We developed tacit knowledge when we were teaching the summer institute together.

We were doing activities with teachers that involved nanotechnology and math. As we conducted each summer institute, we got better at delivering the professional development more efficiently and effectively. When we witnessed firsthand how the tasks played out and how the teachers made sense of the tasks, we adjusted our actions based on our tacit knowledge.

You need knowledge and information to make good decisions. Consider the analogy of making a circuit with a light bulb, batteries, and wires. The flow of electricity is necessary to turn the light bulb on. John Seely Brown and Paul Duguid (2017) point out in *The Social Life of Information*, that learning happens when there is a *need* to use knowledge and information as opposed to force-feeding information.

Learning happens when opportunities are created, and resources are available, according to Brown and Duguid. Therefore, this is something you should consider. Consider what information is needed, how your team can access it, and when it should be available for making decisions.

➤ *Personal relationships make communication easier.*

Dr. Megan Franke points out that the personal relationships that she developed with her team helped generate knowledge. She explained that relationships helped her understand how someone else was thinking and what their perspective was. When someone said something that she disagreed with or did not understand, she was able to ask questions or challenge their thinking by asking for an explanation or providing a counterargument.

She felt that regular face-to-face meetings are valuable. She points out that if you are not in the same room together, this might be a little more challenging. The relationship that you build one-on-one is valuable for having distant conversations. She points out that being in the same room is optimal for discussing things in depth. The reality is that physically getting together is not always possible.

➤ *Timely and relevant information when there is a need makes the workflow easier.*

Having access to information and knowledge available when there is a need makes the workflow much easier. It allows you to make informed decisions at that particular moment in time. Too much information can be overwhelming. Have you ever had days when your inbox is overflowing, and your mailbox is piled up?

You don't have the time and energy to look through everything. When people get information overload, they tend to ignore the information and overlook critical pieces. Therefore, the key is to make sure that the team has access to relevant information when needed to make decisions. This requires thinking about what information is necessary, at what point, and by whom?

Think About . . .

Think about the differences between EXPLICIT knowledge and TACIT knowledge. What kind of knowledge is needed to complete your goals at different stages of the project?

TACIT KNOWLEDGE is part of the social capital of your team. Think about how to share this knowledge with newcomers or across team or organizational boundaries. This is where the role of brokers comes in. A broker is a person who participates in the team and belongs to another community. (Lave and Wenger, 2002)

CREATE A COMMUNICATION PLAN

INTERVIEW WITH MR. PRIYAN FERNANDO

How people interact with each other changes as a project develops. Mr. Priyan Fernando shared the importance of spontaneous and frank communication to generate ideas for innovation.

The ability to speak without constraints and share ideas is an important part of innovation. Mr. Fernando also shared the importance of continuous feedback and constant communication with the team. This feedback allows the team to engage and grow. Furthermore, it also provides timely information and quick decision making as well.

Projects are always evolving, and the context changing. Being able to communicate, adapt, and grow is an important part of innovating. Mr. Fernando shared that digital technology has enabled the use of social media to be used as an effective channel of communication. The convergence of personal and professional lifestyles requires that corporate communication channels be consumerized to be relevant.

He shared that the importance of communication is to "inspire, inform, engage, solicit input and provide feedback on what is working well and what could be improved. Too often informational information gets communicated which leads to overload and lack of action."[1]

> ➤ *Understand the communication networks in a project to evaluate strengths and weaknesses of communication.*

Creating a diagram that shows how the team interacts is helpful to see the big picture of how people connect through networks. An important point to keep in mind is that communication is not static; as the project evolves, the communication dynamics changes as well.

Case Study: Nevada Mathematics Project

The following represents the communication that took place for the summer institutes in the Nevada Mathematics Project. The configuration represents the network of communication in time. As the project evolved so did the communication network.

Communication networks involve thinking about what each group is working on and the flow of communication. We had a core team that traveled and co-taught the sessions. The local organizing teams joined the core team at each location to help co-teach the session.

Therefore, information about what happened in each professional development location was shared among the core professional development team and the local organizing team. The relevant information shared depended on the need at that moment in time. How people participate and the kind of groups that form is *dynamic*. This means that the needs and even the group's configurations change as participation evolves. For example, when the team first met, it was about writing the grant proposal, and most of the project team did this long distance. However, when the work began, we were together for four weeks in the same location.

Not every team member participated in the follow-up session, a smaller core team traveled to each location, and it was one day at a time. The nature of information shared and the dynamics of the groups evolved. There was now a long lapse between follow-up sessions (three per site). However, norms that developed when the smaller core team met influenced how we communicated and interacted. We understood each other's thinking so we could work efficiently and get things done. It was like almost finishing each other's sentences!

Communication, relationships, and the work are dynamic. As time passes and the project and participation evolve, so does the communication. Be mindful throughout the project that things are changing, and make sure that communication is moving along. Mathew Hora and Susan B. Millar (2012), the authors of *A Guide to Building Education Partnerships: Navigating Diverse Cultural Context to Turn Challenge into Promise*, point out that you need to come up with some specific ways to communicate with each other at the beginning of the project. You also need to monitor and adjust as things change.

Think About . . .

- *What kind of information do you need to make decisions?*
- *How are those decisions related to the goals of your project?*
- *How and when should information be available to move the agenda forward?*

➤ *Participation influences how often people communicate and the kind of communication needed.*

The goals of your project and what you are trying to accomplish must drive the kind of conversations that take place. You need to consider at what point of the project people need to come together to step back and reflect and brainstorm ideas on what to do next. Not everyone needs to have every piece of information.

For example, it was not necessary for the local regional teams in the Nevada Mathematics Project to have the attendance and teacher lists from the other sites. However, this information was important for the budget person who needed to know who had to be paid, and at what time, and could answer questions from individual teachers.

Action Items

- Create a graphic that represents the current configuration of groups and networks in your project.
- Think about the lines of communication. What kind of communication is flowing? Is it relevant and timely?
- Are there any hindrances for communication? Think about strategies you could use to keep the information flowing.
- What kind of communication is taking place in each group, and what information needs to be shared?
- Is someone coordinating the flow of information?
- Do people know where to get information and when?
- Do you have a mechanism to share information, such as using technology?
- Create a centralized location to share and find information such as a website.

➤ *Coordinating information across the project to ensure things are moving along is helpful.*

The important part of information sharing is having people responsible for pieces of information and monitoring that the information keeps flowing in the system. If a problem comes up, there needs to be mechanisms for identifying missing information and addressing the situation. Team members should know what their role is in this process. Also, they need to know who to notify or contact if they run into a problem or are unable to follow-through.

Case Study: Nevada Mathematics Project

The Nevada Mathematics Project website became a useful tool to share information. People had a place to figure out dates, locations, times, and other information. It is also a great communication tool to share the work that is going on with the community. Cloud storage such as Dropbox and Google Docs became useful for the exchange of information and storing PowerPoint files and materials in a centralized place.

In this way, people could see what others were working on and had access to common documents and things stored for easy access. Many times, information was shared through emails, phone calls, and so on. Coming up with a system of recording relevant information and taking care of things makes life a lot easier. I found it helpful to create a binder and checklists to keep track of things. That way, all my materials were in one spot. I could refer to Dropbox for more detailed files. Key people in the project were responsible for coordinating different kinds of information.

➤ *Time and distance creates communication challenges.*

Communication is much easier when the team is working closely to-gether. However, when the team is not in the same location, it is much harder to communicate. Therefore, finding ways to communicate and to connect to the "big picture" is important. Project meetings where people gather to share what they have been doing and get on the same page are helpful.

➤ *Use a balanced approach to communication with the micro- and macrolevel with the project team.*

Thinking about the "big picture" of what you are trying to accomplish while working on parts is important. A balanced approach to communica-tion with the team is necessary. Dr. Jbeily (n.d.) shares that the "component of leadership is the ability to see the big picture and being able to push and pull based on the "big picture." Therefore, a balanced approach is needed.

You need to pay attention to what is happening at the big-picture level as well as the microlevel. Dr. Jbeily shares that you can't overdo one and not the other. He points out that if you focus on only the "big picture" or the microlevel, it creates distrust.

Think about how you can balance the micro- and macrolevel communi-cation. The microlevel communication is needed to get things done. The big-picture communication is necessary so that the team sees the entire cathedral and not just its individual stones. However, you need to carve the stone with tools to build the cathedral.

Think About . . .

- *What is the big picture of your project? What needs to be communi-cated?*
- *Who are your stakeholders and end users? What kind of information needs to be communicated? What is your plan? When does the infor-mation need to be communicated?*
- *Timing of communication is important for information to be relevant. Therefore, consider timing when communicating information.*
- *What is your mechanism for communication of unplanned informa-tion that needs to be shared?*

The reality is that time and distance create communication challenges. The bottom line is that people are busy and lack endless time to work on things. What should drive communication are the goals that need to be accomplished.

Action Items
Communication Framework

- What do you need to communicate and how does it relate to your goals?
- Think about the context in which you communicate the information. How will it be received?
- What are some key points that you need to make?
- What information do you need to ask for?
- Listen to others' perspectives and needs, and answer questions.
- Think about how to create a win-win situation where both sides mutually benefit from the conversation.
- What are the concrete action items that need to be addressed?
- How do you plan to keep track of the key points of the conversation for future reference?

SELECT MECHANISMS FOR COMMUNICATION THAT MAKE SENSE

There is no perfect solution for communication. You need to find ways to communicate that fit with what you are trying to accomplish with your team. Do what makes sense for your project. The next section captures how people across different projects communicated. Think about what type of communication makes sense for your project. These ideas might inspire you to think of innovative ways to communicate in your project.

Dr. Mitchell Nathan shared that he conducted regular weekly project meetings at each site. His project involved working with multiple universities that were doing work at their location.

This was different from the Nevada Mathematics Project, where the work with the teachers took place in Nevada. He shared how he communicated with his team. His research team met weekly and each site met weekly at their campus. This was done separately, and then he would coordinate with the project leaders at each location through phone meetings.

He said that they had almost weekly phone meetings such as conference calls for all the sites. If someone could not meet, they just did not go to that meeting. The goal was to get at least an hour in each week. He did mention that one of the challenges was the timing issue. Sometimes they were waiting for a piece of the project from one site so that they could move the work along. He found that the deadlines set by conferences and research projects help keep people stay on track in getting things accomplished.

➤ *The role of a leader is to coordinate, monitor, generate, and disseminate the flow of information and knowledge to keep things moving along.*

➤ *Deadlines are helpful for keeping people on track. Otherwise, work can get backlogged and prevent the workflow.*

BUILD YOUR NETWORK FOR COMMUNICATION

Invest time and build your social network in the community you serve. These relationships are important for you to innovate and provide meaningful work. Relationships do not form through mandates and directives from institutions. Mandates tend to create more resentment than relationships building. For example, an institution may form a partnership with a school and demand that the teachers work with them. However, the reality is that teachers and leaders will only work with you if they feel that you have something to offer and that you care.

Formalized partnerships are useful if they are developed from a bottom-up approach as opposed to top-down. This applies to any group of people you work with or serve. Volunteering time and serving the community are helpful to build trust and relationships.

Genuine friendships are valuable, and trust is something that is earned and cannot be demanded and forced. These are necessary ingredients for building a network to make a difference. Dr. Jbeily shared the importance of establishing relationships with people through personal contact. He visited schools and talked to people. This is something that I did as well. Think about the community that you are serving. Take time to build relationships that matter. This applies to your higher purpose in doing this work.

Dr. Barufaldi shared that building a relationship requires supporting the community and addressing needs. He said that you must improve things by understanding their struggles and needs.

When he went to the schools, he listened to the community to understand their perspective. He treated them as the experts, as opposed to himself. He felt that the community appreciated that. This means you make them the experts, not you, he explained.

> You can't go in and say, "Look this is what is wrong with your community. Here is the white missionary to save you." You have to go in and understand what their problems are, and you have to be sincere about it.

> A lot of researchers go in and take, take, take and don't give anything back into the community. Years ago, I was in Baltimore, and we did research in the schools, we could do anything there because they knew that we would improve the status of learning science education in their schools.

Serving the community, understanding their needs, and developing personal contacts is an important part of building your network to make a difference. I had spent many years traveling across the state of Nevada meeting with people, visiting schools, talking to district leaders and teachers. These relationships have been valuable for serving the needs of the community and developing friendships along the way.

When I first came to Nevada, I had no idea of the geography. Two colleagues and I drove many miles in a pickup truck across the rugged, beautiful Nevada landscape talking to people. When I met people, I made a personal connection that was more than reading about someone on a piece of paper. The warm welcome that I received from teachers and district leaders touched me. I wanted to help and make a difference. They were open and welcoming.

I got a real sense of how geography impacted people's environment. Rural-area teachers drove many miles to attend professional development. This means considering the weather conditions is also important. Understanding the culture of the small towns and the similarities of and differences of them was a valuable experience for me personally.

Visiting schools and classrooms across the state has given me experiences and images that I can draw from so that I can connect with people. I developed a *tacit* understanding of Nevada communities that is hard to understand from only reading reports. Furthermore, it aligned with my mission of being able to serve.

Dr. Barufaldi explained that when his project first got started, the staff would visit every single school they were serving. They would interview the teachers. Now that the project has grown, it has become harder to meet with everyone and is costly too. Now they should think about other creative ways, such as sharing videos or through group meetings, to connect.

Mathew Hora and Susan B. Millar (2012), in *A Guide to Building Education Partnerships*, explain that you need to think about why individuals or organizations would want to partner with you. Understanding the reason helps build a strong partnership. Usually, there is a need for partnering with others.

➤ *Key people in different communities make it easier to get things done!*

Identify key stakeholders in the community that you are serving to be part of your team. These individuals are essential for the success of your project and the ability to work efficiently and get things done. You also have valuable insight into their tacit knowledge of the community that they serve. These key persons are usually in leadership roles. They can communicate with their organizations as well as provide support and resources.

We were fortunate in the Nevada Mathematics Project to work with key district leaders and regional trainers who had excellent communication within the district(s) and had an in-depth understanding of the context of their communities. Building relationships and good communication with the district leaders and the regional trainers are vital to the success of the project.

They have an insider's view of things and can communicate needs. They also act as brokers between your project and the district or the regional training centers. Each organization has its own beliefs and ways of doing things. A broker understands what your project is doing and thinking and can communicate to their community as well as yours.

When you work together, you can accomplish great things by pooling resources and knowledge. Having a broker also becomes a mechanism to share information and knowledge between different communities.

Think About . . .

- *Who are the key people in the communities you serve that have an insider's perspective? These individuals have a great network of communication and have access to resources to support the work of the project.*
- *The relationships between these individuals should be mutually beneficial. They should be part of your team so that everyone learns from one another's expertise.*

CONSIDER THE "BIG PICTURE"

Big picture thinking involves all the people who you are serving as well as those who support you to achieve great things. So, think about our stakeholders, the community you serve, and your team members. Dr. Jbeily shared that seeing the big picture in the community you serve is important. He pointed out that it is so easy to get caught up in work and lose sight of big picture thinking. Therefore, he had multiple venues and mechanisms for communications. Below are examples of what his team did.

➤ *Communicating the value of people's contribution brings good will and makes work visible.*

Teacher Appreciation Annual Meeting

Showing appreciation and honoring people's work is an important part of developing a network. Dr. Jbeily treated teachers who had been working in his project like celebrities. He gave them the red carpet treatment and honored them. He shared with me that "teachers will come crying" because they were so touched. He wanted to make them feel appreciated and valued.

A conference was held with guest speakers and teachers showcasing their work. Donors were invited to this event to be able to witness the return on their investment personally. Having the donor meet with the teachers allowed them to witness how their contributions touched lives personally. It was also an opportunity to honor their support.

Project Directors Meeting

The project team deserves to be recognized and appreciated as well. The Texas Regional Collaboratives had a network of project directors spread out across the state. Every year, a meeting to honor their work and thank them was planned. Sometimes people may have worked in isolation. Bringing people together to honor their work validates the work that has been ongoing; it fosters communication and team spirit.

TELL YOUR STORY!

My father used to say that stories are the most precious heritage of mankind.

— Tahir Shah, *In Arabian Nights*

The big-picture thinking involves sharing with others what you are doing. It involves telling your story. Your story must align with the project goals and how you accomplished various milestones and the people who helped along the way.

CASE STUDY: NEVADA MATHEMATICS PROJECT

We shared our work at the state superintendents meeting and to get their feedback. In addition, we met with Mr. Brian Mitchell at the Nevada governor's office. He shared with me the governor's vision for STEM education, and we cross-linked our websites. The Nevada governor felt that it was important to prepare our students in STEM.

The most important part of sharing your story is sharing your vision and what you have been doing to further the vision of the school districts and state. It is about working together with a shared understanding of what we hope to achieve. The most exciting part is that we officially formalized the Nevada Mathematics Project initiative, and it is now a permanent initiative in the college, and the networks are not formalized. Our goal over time is to build on this work to improve education in Nevada.

Dr. Jbeily also communicated with the legislatures and shared what they were doing. He also met with school boards and parents. Making work visible and getting support helps build on what was being done and sustaining it over time. Texas Regional Collaboratives is a long-standing project at the University of Texas, Austin. The sustainability of the work is dependent on developing networks, finding funding, and doing high-quality work. In Nevada, we just laid the foundation to work together as a state to build a great STEM workforce.

Communicating what you are doing and the impact you are having is valuable. Especially for the people who funded you and supported you. They want to know that you are making a difference and being good stewards of the funding. Dr. Jbeily shared with me that he also communicated with the community by inviting TV, newspaper, and radio interviews.

These were mechanisms to get the word out so that the work received community support. His team developed beautiful colorful brochures that highlighted what they were working on.

> ➤ *Celebrating milestones is an important part of motivation as well as communication.*

Sometimes it is so easy to get caught in the minutia and forget the great work that is being done. I learned that simply keeping an updated website of our efforts gave the project team and the teachers a sense of accomplishment. It is nice to step back and reflect that "wow," we did some "excellent work here."

Celebrations help motivate everyone to keep going even when the work gets hard. Also, it is important to keep the stakeholders, such as the donors, funders, and the community, in the loop. The Texas Regional Collaboratives has a fantastic track record of funding and sustaining the work over time. Their work inspired me to think about how to do this in Nevada. The bottom line is that funding is necessary to do great things! Dr. Barufaldi shared with me how important it is to make the stakeholders, such as the parents and the community, aware of the work you are doing.

INTERVIEW WITH DR. JAMES BARUFALDI

I believe in educating the stakeholders; they are so far removed. The first step is informing the stakeholders. Making them aware and then it goes back into ownership.

CHAPTER SUMMARY

Create Mechanisms for Communication and Knowledge Sharing

> ➤ *Continuous communication with immediate feedback optimizes opportunities to innovate.*

A successful leader is someone who ensures that the team is openly communicating. The communication extends to stakeholders, end users, and donors as well. There are two kinds of knowledge: One is the explicit knowledge that is made up of facts and is easier to share. The other is tacit knowledge that is acquired through experience and knowledge that is harder to share. Tacit knowledge is essential for innovation.

There are several challenges for communication. These include the frequency of meetings, the configurations of groups, and the dynamics and the background of the team members. Communication must extend beyond the team to stakeholders, donors, and end users so that the team can get support and feedback for the innovation. Developing relationships with stakeholders is necessary.

Many forms or modes of communication can be used in a way that makes sense to the project. The important part of sharing knowledge and information is to ensure that it is relevant and available. Creating structures for communicating is helpful. Documenting things in a common place such as a website or cloud drive that the team can access is useful.

The role of a leader is to coordinate, monitor, generate, and disseminate the flow of information and knowledge to keep things moving along.

➤ *Deadlines are helpful for keeping people on track. Otherwise, work can get backlogged and prevent the workflow from moving forword.*

➤ *Identify mechanisms and the nature of communication.*

Two Types of Knowledge

Explicit knowledge: this is information that can be easily shared.

Tacit Knowledge: intuitive understanding of how things function through a combination of experience and knowledge.

STRATEGIES FOR COMMUNICATING EFFECTIVELY WITH TEAMS AND STAKEHOLDERS

CREATE A PLAN FOR THE TEAM TO COMMUNICATE

Evaluate communication needs:

- What kind of information do you need to make decisions?
- How are those decisions related to the goals of your project?
- How would the information be available when needed?
- Create a graphic that represents the current configuration of groups and networks in your project.
  - Think about the lines of communication. What kind of communication is flowing? Is it relevant and timely?
  - Are there any hindrances for communication? Think about strategies you could use to keep the information flowing.

○ What kind of communication is taking place in each group, and what information needs to be shared?
○ Is someone coordinating the flow of information?
○ Create a list of who is responsible for sharing and managing the information. What should team members do if they encounter a problem?

IDENTIFY MECHANISMS FOR COMMUNICATION

- What are your mechanisms for communication: email, Skype, texts, Google Docs, and so on?
- Create a centralized location to share and find information such as a website.

CONSIDER MICRO AND MACRO NEEDS

- What aspect of the project needs to be communicated to stakeholders?
- What is the part of the project that is being worked on at a microlevel that needs to be communicated?
- Who are your stakeholders and end users? What kind of information needs to be communicated? What is your plan? When does the information need to be communicated?
- The timing of communication is important for information to be relevant. Therefore, plan when the information needs to be shared.
- What is your mechanism for communication of unplanned information that needs to be shared?

COMMUNICATE MILESTONES AND SUCCESSES

- Celebrating milestones with the team is motivating because they can see progress.
- Communicate success with stakeholders to get continued support such as funding.

NOTE

1. Interview with Mr. Priyan Fernando conducted by Teruni Lamberg.

5

Moving Forward

Wherever you go, go with all your heart!

—Confucius

Leading a team to innovate involves thinking about where ideas come from and how to generate them. Understanding the creative process and how to devise conditions to innovate is an important part of leading a team for extraordinary results. Many of us do not start out as a leader. However, leadership skills are needed to make a real difference in lives of others and improve the human condition regardless of discipline.

Leading a team to innovate is different from managing. The biggest difference in leading a team to innovate involves generating new ideas and coming up with innovative theories, products, or services to make life better for others. Leading to innovate is different from just maintaining the status quo to keep things running.

The effective leader understands how to structure formal and informal experiences. The informal, free-flowing ideas that get generated are as equally important as the ideas that get developed in formal meetings. An important part of leading productive meetings is to create a nonthreatening environment for the team members to share ideas with one another. Also, the team needs to reflect on one another's ideas and build on them as they relate to the problem.

This type of meeting involves a design process of continually reflecting, refining, and building on ideas. The leader's role is to ensure that these ideas keep moving and people come prepared to share. The leader also ensures that timely and relevant communication is taking place with the team and stakeholders.

A leader who directs a team to innovate is a lifelong learner. Howard Gardner's framework from his book *Five Minds for the Future,* is helpful when thinking about leadership. In his book, he describes "five minds" that are needed for the future so that people can have productive personal and professional lives. They are the *Respectful Mind,* the *Disciplined Mind,* the *Synthesizing Mind,* the *Creating Mind,* and the *Ethical Mind.*

Leading a team to innovate involves the intersection of these minds in two ways: The leader needs to develop the Five Minds of The Future within to be effective. The leader also must create conditions for the team to develop and capitalize on the Five Minds of the Future.

➢ *An Ethical Mind leads to a higher purpose.*

Dr. Gardner shared that the Ethical Mind strives to do good work and engage in good citizenship. The Ethical Mind is needed to come up with a *higher purpose.* The project team must identify a problem in society and find solutions to make things better.

Dr. Gardner points out that this process involves understanding the core values of one's profession. He talks about being a good steward in the face of obstacles and even willing to speak out at a personal cost to be a good steward. Dr. Jbeily advises that in "face of obstacles and adversity, you should never change your principles and goals."

Case Study: Nevada Mathematics Project

> The Nevada Mathematics Project served the entire state of Nevada and all its school districts. It positively impacted more than twelve thousand students. Teachers gained knowledge. The team traveled more than nineteen thousand miles in three years!
>
> Doing this work was physically demanding and time-consuming. There was tension between doing the good work of the project and serving the community while meeting other professional demands. The team held steadfast to the mission of serving the community despite challenges. A higher purpose drove them.

➢ *A Disciplined Mind is needed to think creatively and innovate.*

Leading a team to innovate requires disciplinary and interdisciplinary knowledge and the ability to continue learning. The project team, including the leader, need to have core disciplinary knowledge and an interdisciplinary knowledge. This is because the project team should examine a problem from a 360-degree perspective to come up with creative solutions.

Dr. Gardner points out that people need disciplinary knowledge within a core discipline. Also, they need the ability to acquire interdisciplinary knowledge and continue learning. He also said that people need to develop ways of thinking within the core disciplines.

CASE STUDY: NEVADA MATHEMATICS PROJECT

The goal of the Nevada Mathematics Project was to support teachers to learn geometry and statistics through the context of nanotechnology to support student learning. The kind of knowledge needed to carry out this work included disciplinary knowledge of mathematics, science, cognitive science, mathematics education, and science education.

An interdisciplinary team was necessary to conduct professional development for teachers. The core problem to solve was, "How do we increase teacher content knowledge of core disciplines while supporting them to help their students learn?" The team needed to have a thorough understanding of core knowledge to be able to contribute to the project. Also, we needed to learn from each other and acquire new knowledge. Otherwise, we would not have been able to build on each other's work meaningfully. The project team developed into a *learning team* to carry out the work and innovate.

Developing the *Disciplined Mind* as a leader and a team is a necessary part of finding a solution to a problem from a holistic perspective. An important part of leadership involves carefully selecting an interdisciplinary team to address the problem. Having disciplinary and interdisciplinary knowledge and the ability to learn makes it easier to assemble an interdisciplinary team. The team must continue to learn.

➤ *The Synthesizing Mind is needed to make sense of information.*

An important part of leading a team to innovate involves making sense of what is happening as the project unfolds. Design work is an important part of innovation. It requires asking questions such as: "What is working?" "What is not working, and why?" Structuring project meetings to focus on ideas and examining what is happening is helpful. This process also involves sifting through a lot of information and identifying key findings related to the project goals. This process includes filtering and refining ideas into essential ideas. Once ideas are refined, the team can make decisions needed to make progress toward project goals.

➤ *The Creating Mind and the Respectful Mind are needed to communicate
with each other, generate ideas, and solve problems.*

The purpose of innovation is to make things better, faster, or cheaper.
The *Creating Minds* and *Respectful Minds* are needed for innovation. Dr.
Gardner points out that individuals need to think beyond existing knowledge in powerful ways. People need to be able to come up with creative
solutions that push the boundaries of current knowledge. This is the
whole purpose of leading to innovate. Leading to innovate is the ability
to improve things and make them better. It also involves coming up with
novel solutions.

The leader must structure experiences for the team to create. This
process involves a combination of formal and informal experiences.
The innovative-leader interviews revealed the importance of working
organically and *flexibly* to solve problems. This process involves engaging
in provocative thinking by leveraging resources and solving problems
creatively. Productive discussion is necessary to generate ideas, refine
ideas, and move toward creative solutions.

The *Respectful Mind*, according to Dr. Gardner, involves the ability to
interact with each other in constructive and respectful ways. The leader
must cultivate a culture of respect within the team. This part includes
valuing and honoring people.

Informal experiences allow team members to get to know each other
personally. These relationships are important for sharing ideas and tack-
ling challenging and stressful problems. The *Respectful Mind* should not
only apply to how the team interacts. It should also extend to the community that the team is serving and all stakeholders. A key theme that
emerged from the innovative-leader interviews was the desire to make a
difference!

WHY IT IS IMPORTANT TO CONCEPTUALIZE
A PROBLEM AND ASSEMBLE AN EFFECTIVE TEAM

An important criterion for running a successful project is to identify the
right problem and carefully select team members. *Leaders Who Successfully Lead: Guidelines for Organizing to Achieve Innovation* provides concrete
strategies on how to do this. Applying a creative process to an unrelated
problem and having the wrong people on your team can be a disaster!

A leader should identify his or her higher purpose. This higher purpose and core values should drive the leader's decisions. Conceptualiz-
ing a project that aligns with the leaders' higher values makes the work
meaningful. Furthermore, once a problem is identified, the leader must

carefully select the team by examining the problem from multiple per-spectives. The book describes the process used by innovative leaders to conceptualize problems to solve. The team must clearly understand their individual role and contributions to the project.

Once the team is selected, the leader must co-create the vision with the team to get buy-in and create conditions to generate ideas. The book outlines the role of a leader. The leader's knowledge and experiences are important for leading a team. The leader takes on a role as a coach and a co-learner and empowers team to take initiative. The intricacies of how innovative leaders do this is described. In addition, it describes how the innovative leaders create a nonthreatening environment to empower the team to explore ideas and innovate.

START SMALL AND SCALE-UP

> The world of reality has its limits, the world of imagination is bound-less.
>
> —Jean-Jacques Rousseau

Starting at a smaller scale, learning from that experience, and then scaling-up is helpful. When you do things at a more minor level, you gain experience and valuable tacit knowledge.

CASE STUDY: NEVADA MATHEMATICS PROJECT

> My experience in running the Northeastern Nevada Mathematics Project that served the northeastern region in the state was valu-able for conceptualizing the statewide project. I learned what was involved in running a project in Nevada. I learned what to anticipate and things I should think about. Over the years, I built up relation-ships and networks. Furthermore, my work in the Northeastern Nevada Mathematics Project built on the work that I did with Dr. Cobb as a postdoc at Vanderbilt.

SEEK MENTORS WHO CAN PROVIDE SUPPORT

Mentors are very helpful when you are facing obstacles or learning how to run a project. This is one of the reasons I wrote this book. The people that I interviewed for this book are my mentors. You can learn great things from people who have done great things. Who are your mentors? What kind of mentoring do you need to run your project? What skills do you need to develop so that you can be a successful leader who can guide a team to innovate for impact? The next section provides insights from K–12 innovative educators in the field. They share their stories and the lessons learned about leading teams.

VOICES FROM THE FIELD: INNOVATIVE K–12 LEADER INTERVIEWS

This section contains interviews with K–12 innovative leaders. Their work has made a significant impact in their respective communities. The interviews reflect experiences and insights gained by these leaders in the field. The principles outlined in this book can be used in any setting to lead a team to solve a problem and innovate, not just education. The interviews represent just one context.

HOW TO ENGAGE A TEAM IN CREATIVE PROBLEM SOLVING

Engage in Creative Problem Solving by Capitalizing on Team Expertise

Building on individual strengths yields creative solutions and team spirit.

Lamberg: What strategies do you use in your meetings to make sure you capitalize on the teams' expertise?

Interview with Mr. David Ebert, Oregon High School Math Teacher/ Leadership Team, Oregon, Wisconsin, NCTM Board Member

➤ *Shared responsibility builds intellectual community.*

I have worked with many different principals on our school's Leadership Team. One, in particular, believed very strongly in top-down decision making and management. When he led our building and our Leadership Team, we accomplished the tasks we needed to complete, but it felt very much like checking boxes off a list. There was no innovation, creativity, or deviation from the list. On the other hand, when there has been shared responsibility as part of our Leadership Team, the group has operated like an intellectual community.

Education is a complex endeavor. Top-down management can accomplish tasks, even complicated tasks; but solving complex educational problems requires the thinking and leadership of the entire team.

➤ *Providing wait time affords opportunities for reflection.*

I rely on wait time. I find if I speak up too much, then the group will just follow my ideas as the "leader" and I don't get the level of input I'm looking for. Conversely, if I wait after someone speaks, another person in the group will chime in to build off the ideas presented or present an additional perspective. Wait again, and the chain of shared wisdom continues. This way I can facilitate and be an active listener learning alongside the entire team, which is way more fun and inspiring!

HOW TO RUN MEETINGS TO
MOVE PROJECT AGENDA FORWARD

The Journey of Ideas to Theory and Products Requires Action

Teams can adapt and adjust action items to fit with big picture.

Lamberg: What do you do to move ideas forward?

INTERVIEW WITH MS. HOLLY MARICH, REGIONAL TRAINER, NORTHEASTERN NEVADA PROFESSIONAL DEVELOPMENT PROGRAM, ELY, NEVADA

➤ *Being reflective, aware of how others see you, and learning from that reality.*

When I first started teaching, I was not young, but I was naïve. I already had a bachelor's degree in elementary education, a master's degree in curriculum and instruction, and I had been a stay-at-home mom for seven years. While staying home with my three small children, I also substitute taught, tutored, volunteered at our local library, and taught summer school. I was coming into full-time teaching feeling like I knew something. This confidence in myself was not well received. I thought the teachers I worked with thought about and cared about educational issues as I had. I also thought they were interested in discussing educationally related topics like extrinsic rewards and tracking.

So, when I shared articles and wanted to discuss best practices in teaching, I had no idea I was offending my colleagues. I was so naïve! My first year of teaching concluded with my formal evaluation naming me as arrogant and disrespectful toward teachers with more experience. It wasn't until this evaluation that I learned I was offending my colleagues. I was so embarrassed, ashamed, and upset. I thought I knew something about teaching when really, I only knew something about pedagogy. I quickly learned how complex and difficult the whole of what it means to be a teacher can be. I came to realize the political aspect of education.

The politics of my district and the politics of my school. Learning from my mistakes and unguided choices, I started to think carefully about how my words would be interpreted by the people around me. I started to think about how to invite teachers into conversations about teaching in a way that would not offend them. During my second year of teaching, I decided to stop talking about what I was thinking or doing with my teaching unless someone asked me first. I found when a colleague initiated the conversation this was the best way to engage without offending. Over time, people started asking about what I was doing and why I was doing it, and I eventually established myself as an educational leader among my colleagues.

I am grateful that I noticed early on how to better invite colleagues into conversations about teaching, questioning why we do what we do and why we believe what we believe.

INTERVIEW WITH MS. SAMANTHA WUTTING, K–12 MATH MENTOR TEACHER, SPECIAL EDUCATION, FAIRBANKS NORTH STAR BOROUGH DISTRICT, ALASKA

➤ *Moving forward involves accepting that the ideas you present may not be where you end up.*

Moving ideas forward is to have the acceptance that the ideas that you present may not be where you end up with the group you are leading. There are many instances where I have led groups and we end up going someplace else that is just as valuable. I have the momentum of the group going that way. If I were to stick to my idea of where we were going, it would not go very far. I would not have the investment from the group. In Alaska, we are trying to reach out to rural members of Alaska Council of Teachers of Mathematics.

One question we have is how can we provide professional development for teachers in remote sites that are only accessible by plane? My original idea was to have monthly webinars by one of our members to teachers in remote sites. Alaska Council of Teachers of Mathematics members would be able to access grade-level resources related to the webinar. Through discussions, we are now considering coaching for members. This is not what I envisioned when I started, but I believe it has become a better model for us to pursue.

HOW TO CONSIDER END USERS'
NEEDS WHEN TESTING AND REFINING DESIGN

Engage in Provocative Thinking

➤ *Opportunity to leverage resources and creatively problem solve for innovation.*

Lamberg: Give an example of how you leveraged resources (material or intellectual) to enhance the work of your project. What did you learn in the process?

INTERVIEW WITH MR. DAVID EBERT, OREGON HIGH SCHOOL MATH TEACHER/ LEADERSHIP TEAM, OREGON, WISCONSIN, NCTM BOARD MEMBER

➤ *Prioritizing helps focus on the "customer."*

Our school has an Instructional Leadership Team composed of teachers, administrators, and key building leaders. We recently read the book *Five Levers to Improve Learning* by Tony Frontier and James Rickabaugh. The book presents three critical questions for prioritizing efforts to improve student learning, and we try to use these questions to guide our work. The questions are: 1. What is the student outcome we are trying to influence? 2. What will have the most direct impact on influencing that outcome for students? 3. Does the change require a transactional change in process or a transformational change in thought and practice?

This prioritizing focuses our team's work on the "customer"—our students.

INTERVIEW WITH MS. MARISSA MCCLISH, STUDENT LEARNING OBJECTIVE COORDINATOR, WASHOE SCHOOL DISTRICT, RENO, NEVADA

➤ *Continue to develop and grow as a leader and gain knowledge and skills!*

The art of working with people is something that you can improve upon. "Important to be an active consumer of different strategies." Hoping to coach people and bring ideas out and put my words into my thoughts. Learning to coach people into coming into their own realization and points of growth and constantly reflecting upon own improvement. How can I make this more acceptable, engaging and relevant and help me to work with different group of people? I don't want to walk in as an expert, and I want to increase my, expertise in every group I am working on. I must learn to facilitate. People want to follow when they are valued and when they know they have a space to add to the conversation.

HOW TO COMMUNICATE
EFFECTIVELY WITH TEAM AND STAKEHOLDERS

Create Mechanisms for Communication and Knowledge Sharing

➤ *Continuous communication with immediate feedback optimizes opportunities to innovate.*

Lamberg: What are some ways you communicate with your team and stakeholders? What recommendations and suggestions do you have?

INTERVIEW WITH MS. HOLLY MARICH, REGIONAL TRAINER, NORTHEASTERN NEVADA PROFESSIONAL DEVELOPMENT PROGRAM, ELY, NEVADA

➤ *An investment in myself as an educator has been an investment in leadership development.*

➤ *You should be aware of traditions about whose voice seems to matter in education and not let it define you, or perpetuate that tradition.*

I developed my skill in being very careful about communicating why I was doing what I was doing and why I believed what I believed. I no longer assumed others shared in my knowledge or beliefs. I respected my colleagues, and I wanted their respect in return. It was a very fine balance, being new to a community of educators but also being ambitious about change.

Persevering through the "red-tape" to send myself to the IRA conference made me realize how a school or district will often tell you that you can't do something, but when that "something" is worth fighting for, a solution can be found. My approach involved respecting the leadership around me but also not taking no for an answer. I would find the way to make whatever it was happening if it was something I believed to be important. Over the years I continued to create a reputation for myself as an educator committed to learning, working hard, and being kind and respectful to others. I believe, because of this reputation, I was asked to be part of the Northern Nevada Math Project that led to my second master's degree in education and my connection with the author of this book.

Eventually, through the encouragement and support of district leaders, I successfully applied for a regional professional development position with the Northeastern Nevada Regional Professional Development Program. I continue to invest time and money into my growth as a professional and educational leader through a PhD program in educational psychology and educational technology. I firmly believe I have invested wisely over the years of my career in education and my investments have paid off over and over again.

INTERVIEW WITH MS. JILL ROSS, PRINCIPAL, ALPINE ACADEMY

➤ *Communicate with each other by focusing on the positive in thoughts and actions.*

I believe that we are always positive. We don't talk bad about our students. We discuss what students need and what steps we can take to help them. *Positivity* makes a huge difference! When we meet and talk, it is always student-centered, with each of us asking how we can make a difference. We as leaders also look at the teachers as we look at the students. We ask ourselves, what can we do to make a difference so they have the positive support they need? The growth mindset works for all of us. This, in turn, sets the stage for a positive school culture and student love of learning.

INTERVIEW WITH MS. SAMANTHA WUTTING, K–12 MATH MENTOR TEACHER, SPECIAL EDUCATION, FAIRBANKS NORTH STAR BOROUGH DISTRICT, ALASKA

➤ *Face-to-Face communications provides opportunities to understand another person's nonverbal communication.*

One of my formative experiences for understanding communication came from the National Academy for Science and Mathematics Education Leadership. In our first academy, we played "The Change Game," or Making Change Happen, which is partially based on the concerns-based adoption model. One thing that struck me playing the research-based game is how much we needed to communicate ideas and thoughts to others. By playing this game, I became more aware of how many different people I needed to talk to and how much I need to talk to them to get an idea accepted. Just because an idea is not accepted when you initially talk to people does not mean that the idea is not going to happen. I am also more aware that I need to find a variety of ways to communicate with people, especially today.

I think one of my strengths is that I try to communicate with people in person, which offers me the opportunity to listen and to observe. Looking at the research, nonverbal communication contributes anywhere from 55 percent to 93 percent of a message. The only way to observe the nonverbal communication is by in-person interactions. I became aware of the importance of nonverbal communication through another academy from the National Academy for Science and Mathematics Education Leadership. If I can talk with someone in person, I think that is more effective than sending an email. It allows me to hear and see the impact of my message and provide feedback for me to decide my next steps.

INTERVIEW WITH MR. DAVE BRANCAMP, DIRECTOR, STANDARDS AND
INSTRUCTIONAL SUPPORT, NEVADA DEPARTMENT OF EDUCATION

> *Collaborative efforts build over time, so do relationships and networks ("Who we were back then is not the same as who are today, our positions change, our interactions change, our relationships and collaborative efforts are always evolving"). Effective collaborations are built on a vision, communication, and action over time. Even when people are not directly collaborating, we are engaging in projects that build on a larger vision for a greater good.*

Note: Mr. Brancamp refers to collaboration in the Northeastern Nevada Mathematics Project with the author that took place over ten years ago.

Collaborative efforts build over time. Over a given period of time, you will want to build a sense of trust for those around your team and come to a consensus on a general vision of the work and goals to meet this vision. Think back to where we started in the rural areas of Nevada and where you have taken the Nevada Math Project today. It is not the same place as where we are now; we all have adapted to our teachers, our students. I remember spending over two hours debriefing and planning for the next session just so the team can become much stronger and the product more refined.

The teachers did not know us. They came with some perceptions of the fear of titles and yet over time came to the realization that we honestly do care about the actual students in the seats. As the representative from NDE, they associated me with rules, regulations, and testing. You were part of the ivory tower. We had to break down these barriers and misconceptions.

The team under your guidance and leadership persevered to the next level even in the face of logistical, financial, and perception difficulties and obstacles. We continued to touch base and remained committed to the overall goal of improving instruction for Nevada students. The team knew we had people behind the goal and we could secure funding to develop a sustainable leadership cadre to rally this work forward. Now we have a leadership network, which allows us to deal with challenging topics of great mathematics instruction.

K–12 INNOVATIVE LEADER BIOGRAPHIES

MR. DAVE BRANCAMP, Director of Standards and Instructional Support, Nevada Department of Education, Carson City, Reno

Mr. Brancamp is currently the director of the Standards and Instructional Supports Office at the Nevada Department of Education (NDE).

Prior to this position, he worked as the director of the Northwest Regional Professional Development Program in Nevada. Preceding his return to the NDE, he was the state math consultant for grades K–12, a principal at a K–8 school, and a mathematics/science teacher for more than fifteen years, mainly in the middle school grades. Most of his current work is spent in the world of academic standards development and revision, and supporting instruction with technical assistance for both administrators and teachers around effective, sustainable leadership for student learning in Nevada.

However, his greatest joy comes from the following: on October 10, he will celebrate thirty years of marriage to his wife Tami, who is a professor at the University of Nevada, Reno, in speech pathology. They are both proud parents of Christopher, who is a sophomore in the TMCC + SNC Entrepreneurial Program.

MR. DAVID EBERT, High School Math Teacher/Leadership Team Member/NCTM Board Member, Oregon, Wisconsin

Mr. Ebert is a mathematics teacher at Oregon High School in southern Wisconsin, and a member of his school's leadership team. He has been teaching students in grades 6–12 for more than twenty years. He is the past president of the Wisconsin Mathematics Council and serves on the board of directors of the National Council of Teachers of Mathematics, and has held multiple leadership roles in both organizations. He has led workshops for teachers on a variety of topics at the local, state, and national level. He is a past recipient of a Kohl Fellowship, the Marquette University School of Education Young Alumnus of the Year Award, a Best Buy Teach award, and the Miriam Connellan Mathematics Education Award. He was recently honored as a Wisconsin Mathematics Council Distinguished Mathematics Educator.

MS. HOLLY MARICH, Professional Development Regional Coordinator, Northeastern Nevada Regional Professional Development Program, Ely, Nevada

Over the past twenty-three years, Holly has been an educator in many capacities: a parent volunteer, substitute teacher, summer school teacher, and full-time elementary school teacher. She is currently a regional coordinator at the Northeastern Nevada Regional Professional Development Program in Nevada. She works with teachers across the northeastern region of the state around topics of literacy and technology. She is also currently a PhD candidate at Michigan State University in the Educational Psychology and Educational Technology, EPET hybrid program.

In addition to her work at MSU, Holly serves on the executive committee as director of membership for the Action Research Network of the

Americans. She has won numerous awards: Literacy Research Association's Dissertation Proposal Mentoring Pre-Conference Program, White Pine County School District Elk's Teacher of the Month May, Vietnam Fellowship to Enhance Global Awareness, Michigan State University College of Education, Nevada Association of School Boards Innovative Teacher of the Year 2011, and Lincoln Highway Historical Society Teacher of the Year 2005.

MS. MARISSA MCCLISH, Student Learning Objective Coordinator, Washoe School District, Reno, Nevada

Marissa taught high school math and science in Ann Arbor, Michigan, and San Francisco, California, before working outside of the classroom in northern Nevada. In Nevada, she helped launch a school-wide STEM program while serving as a middle school instructional coach and has served as a regional educational trainer in six school districts. Her primary passion and work outside of the classroom has focused on the accessibility of quality instruction for all students and empowering teachers to bring engaging, student-driven pedagogy to their classrooms.

Marissa holds a BS in engineering in atmospheric, oceanic, and space sciences and an MEd in Curriculum and Instruction. She is currently working as a district administrator in the Washoe County School District Department of Assessment. Marissa has been active in Math Circles and is currently serving as co-president of the Northern Nevada Math Council. She has spoken at national meetings for the National Council of Teachers of Math and Student Achievement Partners. She continues to be driven by the belief that education is the most complex profession out there and inspired by the continual learning that the field offers.

MS. JILL ROSS, Principal Alpine Academy College Prep High School, Sparks, Nevada

Ms. Ross is the principal of Alpine Academy College Prep High School, located in Sparks, Nevada. She, along with the vice principal are the original founders. Mrs. Ross started her career in education in a small charter school as a social studies and health teacher. She then taught in the local district while she earned her master's in education administration and supervision. Next, she worked as an instructional coach in the district before opening Alpine Academy in 2009. Her school's growth from a 42 percent graduation rate its first year to a 100 percent graduation rate by year five was accomplished with an outstanding team. Ms. Ross was awarded the Charter School Principal of the Year in 2015 and attributed it to a positive culture and strong work ethic at Alpine Academy.

MS. SAMANTHA WUTTIG, K–12 Math Special Education Coach, Fairbanks, Alaska

Ms. Wutting is a K–12 math special education coach working for the Fairbanks North Star Borough School District in Fairbanks, Alaska. Currently, she is the president of the Alaska Council of Teachers of Mathematics and the State Team Leader for Alaska of the National Council of Supervisors of Mathematics. She was the 2012 Iris Carl Grand awardee and participated in WestEd's National Academy for Science and Education Leadership from 2005 to 2007. In 2002, she was the President Awardee of Excellence in Mathematics and Science Teaching.

INNOVATIVE LEADER BIOGRAPHIES

JAMES BARUFALDI, PhD

Professor emeritus, former director, Center for STEM Education, The University of Texas at Austin, a consultant on developing partnerships and STEM education. Dr. James P. Barufaldi was the Ruben E. Hinojosa Regents Professor at the University of Texas at Austin and served as the director of the Center for STEM Education. He also served as principal investigator of the Texas Regional Collaboratives for Excellence in Science Teaching. He served as co-director of the UTeach Secondary Science and Mathematics Teacher Preparation Program. He has supervised more than sixty dissertations and theses in science education.

Dr. Barufaldi was instrumental in developing STEM education at The University of Texas and has an impressive record of scholarship. He directed numerous federally funded projects such as the U.S. Department of Education Project—General Science Content and Inquiry Skills Improvement Program, the Title II funded Coordinated Thematic Science In-service Program, Science Content Improvement Program, the Texas Elementary Science In-Service Program, and the NSF Project ESTT, Empower Science Teachers of Texas. Dr. Barufaldi's research program involved areas of professional development, curriculum design, instructional strategies, and science education. He is known for building strong collaborations within the education community in Texas.

Dr. Barufaldi was selected as a member of the Academy of Distinguished Teachers at the University of Texas at Austin in 2003. He was named a Minnie Stevens Piper Professor, 2002, for "dedication to the teaching profession" as well as "outstanding academic, scientific, and scholarly achievement." He served as president of the National Association for Research in Science Teaching, among others. He also received the 2002 Outstanding Scholar in Education Award presented by the Alumni

Association, College of Education, at the University of Maryland, College Park, and received an honorary doctor of science degree from Marietta College (Ohio) and the Texas Excellence Teaching Award in the College of Education at the University of Texas.

Currently, he is active internationally as a STEM consultant and is investigating the process of building successful collaboratives in the global STEM education community including variables which may contribute to high intensity, sustained collaboration.

PAUL COBB, PhD

Dr. Paul Cobb is a renowned professor in mathematics education at Vanderbilt University. He was awarded the Joe B. Wyatt Distinguished University Professor at Vanderbilt University. His work has earned him numerous awards and honors.

These awards and honors include Sir Alan Newell Visiting Fellowship, Griffith University, Brisbane, Australia, Invited Fellow, Center for Advanced Studies in Behavioral Science. He was inducted into the National Academies and is a member. He is also an Invited Fellow of the Center for Advanced Studies in the behavioral sciences.

Dr. Cobb was awarded the Hans Freudenthal Medal for cumulative research programs over the prior ten years from the International Commission on Mathematics Instruction in 2005. He is a founding class member at the American Education Research Association.

He won the University of Georgia College of Education Lifetime Achievement Alumni Award and the Sylvia Scribner Award for a program of work conducted within the ten years that represents a significant advancement in our understanding of learning and instruction, 2010. He was recently awarded the honor of a distinguished scholar at the American Education Research Association Special Interest Group for Research in Mathematics Education.

Dr. Cobb has served as a principal investigator on numerous grants. His research interests focus on instructional design, issues of equity in mathematics teaching and learning, and the improvement of mathematics teaching on a large scale. Dr. Cobb's current research examines making instructional improvement of mathematics at scale.

A book edited by Erna Yackel, Koeno Gravemeijer, and Anna Sfard that describes the evolution of his research program was published in 2010: *A Journey in Mathematics Education Research: Insights from the Research of Paul Cobb*. He is a co-editor of *Improving Access to Mathematics: Diversity and Equity in the Classroom* and *Symbolizing* and *Communicating in Mathematics Classrooms: Perspectives on Discourse, Tools and Instructional Design*. In addition, he co-edited *The Emergence of Mathematical Meaning: interaction in Classroom Cultures* with Heinrich Bauersfeld.

MR. PRIYAN FERNANDO

Priyan Fernando is the chairman of Brandix Lanka, Ltd. He also works as a senior advisor to the Boston Consulting Group (BCG), one of the most prestigious global consulting firms based in the United States. He consults on corporate governance and business transformation to leading organizations around the world. Priyan recently retired after a distinguished thirty-two-year career with American Express in New York City.

Most recently he was executive vice president, Global Business Services of American Express (AXP), where he was responsible for all internal operations of this $32 billion financial enterprise with a presence in over 130 markets. Priyan's work has resulted in several innovations, including proprietary new ways to drive efficiencies and enhance effectiveness, which have been replicated across American Express and other organizations.

He is using this experience to help leading companies improve their effectiveness in delivering outcomes. Prior to this role, Priyan was president, and chief operating officer of American Express Global Business Travel, where he had P&L responsibility of more than $1 billion and oversaw a staff of over twelve thousand people.

He led a transformation of the Global Service Delivery Network and client management activities across the business and was recognized in the Business Travel World Top 50 newsmakers in 2008. Previously, Priyan served as senior vice president and chief financial officer of American Express Global Corporate Services and was a member of the company's Senior Finance Leadership Team.

In 1994, he was instrumental in introducing Business Process Outsourcing (BPO) in India by pioneering the financial shared services model at American Express. Before joining American Express in 1982, Priyan had a successful public accounting career with Ernst & Young in New York City and prior to that with Ernst & Young in Sri Lanka. Priyan has served on the boards of the New York City Leadership Center, the Advisory Council of the Conference Board and Rearden Commerce.

Priyan is a fellow member of the Institute of Chartered Accountants of Sri Lanka and Chartered Management Accountants of the UK, where he served on the International Committee. He is also a member of the New York Society of Certified Public Accountants. He holds an MBA from Indiana University. His membership in the Global 50 Chief Operating Officers and experience as a senior advisor have given him exposure to best practices across many leading companies. Priyan spends his time in New York and Sri Lanka where he also advises the government of Sri Lanka.

MEGAN FRANKE, PhD

Dr. Megan Franke is an education professor at the Graduate School of Education and Information Studies at UCLA. Dr. Franke served as director of UCLA's Center X from 2001–2008, chair of the UCLA Department of Education from 2008–2013, and as interim dean of GSE&IS in 2012.

She has won numerous awards and has been recognized for her work. She was recently appointed to the National Academies. Dr. Franke, along with her colleagues, was honored with the AERA Henry T. Truba Award for Research Leading to the Transformation of the Social Context in Education along with AERA's Relating Research to Practice Award. She serves as a member at-large at the AERA Council and a member of the AERA executive board.

Dr. Franke's research focuses on understanding and supporting teacher learning for both pre-service and in-service teachers. She studies how teaching mathematics with attention to students and their mathematical thinking can create opportunities for low-income students of color to learn mathematics with understanding. She is known for her leadership in Center X: Where Research and Practice Intersect for Urban School Professionals and her ongoing professional development work to support teachers, schools, and communities.

Dr. Franke has coauthored several books: *Children's Mathematics, Second Edition: Cognitively Guided Instruction; Young Children's Mathematics: Cognitively Guided Instruction in Early Childhood Education; Thinking Mathematics: Integrating Arithmetic & Algebra in Elementary School;* and *Children's Mathematics: Cognitively Guided Instruction.*

ROCHELLE GUTIÉRREZ, PhD

Dr. Gutiérrez is professor of curriculum and instruction and Latina/Latino studies at the University at Illinois at Urbana-Champaign. She has won numerous awards for her work in social justice in mathematics education. She has earned the Excellence in Research Award from the Association of Mathematics Teacher Educators for the work she has conducted and the theories on equity she has offered to the field.

Pace University recognized her as a Distinguished Educator in the Pedagogy of Success in Urban Schools. And, TODOS Mathematics for All awarded her the Iris M. Carl Equity and Leadership Award. Her work has been published in such journals as *American Educational Research Journal, Mathematical Thinking and Learning, Journal for Research in Mathematics Edu-*

cation, Harvard Educational Review, Democracy and Education, Urban Review,
and *Mathematics Teacher.*

She has served as a member of the writing team for the Standards
for Preparing Teachers of Mathematics produced by the Association of
Mathematics Teacher Educators. On a Fulbright fellowship, she studied
secondary mathematics teachers in Zacatecas, México, where she was
able to document the different cultural practices and algorithms used in
Mexican classrooms.

Dr. Gutiérrez's research interrogates the unearned privilege that
mathematics holds in society and the roles that race, class, language, and
gender play in teaching and learning mathematics so as to open up a new
possible relationship between living beings, mathematics, and the planet.

Her current research projects include: theorizing the roles of mathematics in relation to power, identity, the body, and authority in society;
supporting mathematics teachers who engage their students in rigorous
and creative mathematics and who are committed to social justice; and
documenting moments of "Nepantla" and "creative insubordination"
in the everyday practices of mathematics teachers. She is writing a book
called the *Mirror Test.*

KAMIL A. JBEILY, PhD

Dr. Kamil A. Jbeily is currently president of Reach the Stars Enterprise:
Leadership, Partnerships, and Systemic Reform. Dr. Jbeily was born in
Beirut, Lebanon. Completing a BS in chemistry and a masters of science in
chemistry and chemistry education, Kamil taught in the Lebanese secondary schools. In 1980, he immigrated to the United States to attend the University of Texas at Austin, where he earned his PhD in science education.

In 1986, Dr. Jbeily joined the Texas Education Agency (TEA), first as
a science specialist, then as director of science projects. In 1991, Kamil
founded the Texas Regional Collaboratives for Excellence in Science and
Mathematics Teaching (TRC). Under his leadership, this joint initiative of
TEA, UT, Austin, and multiple corporations, grew into a dynamic, statewide network of P–16 partnerships that has improved the knowledge,
skills, and performance of more than fifty thousand teachers of science
and mathematics, and benefited the learning of more than three million
students.

Dr. Jbeily founded the Texas Regional Collaboratives based a statewide
need to improve science education. He did this by initiating a series of
regional meetings across the state to explore ways to create support systems of professional development for Texas science teachers. The meetings included representatives from education service centers, colleges

and universities, school districts, business and industry, and institutions of informal education.

The goal was to create regional partnerships built on collaboration and cost sharing that provided science teachers with relevant, sustained, and high-intensity professional development. These P–16 partnerships, with initial federal funding from the Dwight D. Eisenhower Science Professional Development Program, developed into the statewide network that is now the Texas Regional Collaboratives for Excellence in Science and Mathematics Teaching.

This program won numerous awards. In 2000, Dr. Jbeily was inducted into the Texas Science Hall of Fame, and the governor, the Senate, and the House of Representatives recognized the program for its distinguished achievements and contributions for supporting educational reform.

Dr. Jbeily has always been an active educator. He has never lost touch with the classroom; he served as adjunct professor of chemistry at Austin Community College from 1985–2015. As well, he is a sought-after motivational speaker, having made more than two hundred presentations in the United States and internationally on leadership, excellence, equity, diversity, systemic reform, and founding and sustaining partnerships.

H. RICHARD MILNER IV, PhD

H. Richard Milner IV is the Helen Faison Endowed Chair of Urban Education, professor of education, as well as the director of the Center for Urban Education at the University of Pittsburgh. Dr. Milner is a Fellow of the American Educational Research Association and the recipient of the National Association of Multicultural Education's Carl A. Grant Multicultural Research Award.

He was honored with the John Dewey Award for relating research to practice and the Innovations in Diversity, Teaching, and Teacher Education Award from Division K of the American Educational Research Association. His research, teaching, and policy interests include urban teacher education, African American literature, and the social context of education. In particular, Dr. Milner's research examines policies and practices that support teacher success in urban schools.

His research has been recognized by the American Association of Colleges for Teacher Education's 2012 Outstanding Book Award and the American Education Studies Association's Critic's Choice Book Award for the widely read book, *Start Where You Are but Don't Stay There: Understanding Diversity, Opportunity Gaps, and Teaching in Today's Classrooms.* His most recent book is *Rac(e)ing to Class: Confronting Poverty and Race in Schools and Classrooms.*

MITCHELL J. NATHAN, PhD

Dr. Nathan is Professor of Learning Science in the Department of Educational Psychology at the University of Wisconsin, Madison. He is also the director of the Center on Education and Work and director of the IES Post-Doctoral Fellowship program in Mathematical Thinking, Learning and Instruction. He holds faculty appointments in the Department of Curriculum and Instruction, the Psychology Department and the Wisconsin Center for Education Research (WCER).

He is also a member of the University of Wisconsin Cognitive Science Cluster and the Delta Program Steering Committee. He served as the chair of the Learning Sciences Program from 2004–2010. Dr. Nathan has an impressive record of external funding and publications. He has garnered over $25 million dollars in funding. He was inducted into the Teaching Academy at the University of Wisconsin in 2014 and received Exceptionality Designation at the Department of Educational Psychology at the University of Wisconsin in 2009.

Some of Dr. Nathan's current affiliations include the National Academy of Sciences (NAS) Space Studies Board and National Research Council (NRC) Board of Science Education—Planning Committee for Sharing the Adventure with the Student: Exploring Intersections of NASA Space Science and Education, the National Academy of Engineering (NAE) Committee on Integrated STEM Education, the Institute for (P–12) Engineering Research and Learning—INSPIRE, the Latin American School for Education, Cognitive and Neural Science, Universidad de Chile, Universidad de Buenos Aires, ELS International Institute of Neuroscience and Natal-Brazil, the American Education Research Association, the American Society of Engineering Education, the Cognitive Science Society and the National Council of Teachers of Mathematics, and the International Society of the Learning Sciences, a professional community of scholars who take an interdisciplinary approach to the study of learning, for which he was a founding officer.

Bibliography

Alguezaui, Salma, and Raffaele Filieri. "A Knowledge-Based View of the Extending Enterprise for Enhancing a Collaborative Innovation Advantage." *International Journal of Agile Systems and Management* 7, no. 2 (2014): 116–31.

Alguezaui, Salma and Raffaele Filieri. "Investigating the Role of Social Capital in Innovation: Sparse Versus Dense Network." *Journal of Knowledge Management*, 14, no. 6 (2010): 891

Amabile, Teresa. "Motivating Creativity in Organizations: On Doing What You Love and Loving What You Do." *California Management Review* 40, no. 1 (1997): 39–58.

Belsky, Scott. *Making Ideas Happen: Overcoming the Obstacles between Vision and Reality.* Portfolio, the Penguin Group: New York, 2012.

———. "Knowledge and Organization: A Social-Practice Perspective." *Organization Science* 12, no. 2 (2001): 198–213.

Brown, John Seely, and Paul Duguid. *The Social Life of Information.* Updated, with a new preface. Boston: Harvard Business Review Press, 2017.

Carpenter, Tom, Elizabeth Fennema, Megan Loef Franke, Linda Levi, and Susan B. Empson. *Children's Mathematics, Cognitively Guided Instruction*, revised edition. Portsmouth, NH: Heinemann, 2015.

Christensen, Clayton M. *The Innovator's Dilemma: When New Technologies Cause Great Firms to Fail.* Boston: Harvard Business Review Press, 2013.

Covey, Steve. *The 8th Habit: From Effectiveness to Greatness.* New York: Free Press, 2005.

Csikszentmihalyi, Mihaly. *Creativity: Flow and the Psychology of Discovery and Invention.* New York: HarperCollins, 1996.

Davenport, Thomas H., and Laurence Prusak. *Working Knowledge: How Organizations Manage What They Know.* Boston: Harvard Business School Press, 1998.

Doyle, Charlotte L. "The Creative Process: Effort and Effortless Cognition." *Journal of Cognitive Education and Psychology* 15, no. 1 (2016): 37. DOI: 10.189V1945-8959.15.1.24.

Dweck, Carol S. *Mindset: The New Psychology of Success.* New York: Random House, 2006.

Gardner, Howard. *Five Minds for the Future.* Boston: Harvard Business Review Press, 2009.

———. *Leading Minds.* New York: Basic Books, 1995.

Giaccardi, Elisa, and Gerhard Fischer. "Creativity and Evolution: A Metadesign Perspective." *Digital Creativity* 19, no. 1 (2008): 19–32. DOI: 10.1080/14626260701847456.

Graham-Leviss, Katherine. "The Five Skills that Innovative Leaders Have in Common." *Harvard Business Review*, December 16, 2016, online version. https://hbr.org/2016/12/the-5-skills-that-innovative-leaders-have-in-common.

Guilford, J. P. "Three Faces of Intellect." *American Psychologist* 14, no. 8 (1959): 469–79.

Hora, Matthew T., and Susan B. Millar. *A Guide to Building Education Partnerships: Navigating Diverse Cultural Contexts to Turn Challenge into Promise.* Sterling, VA: Stylus Publishing, 2012.

Jbeily, Kamil. *Transforming the Culture of Education in the United States: Our Future Depends on It.* Institute for Systematic Leadership (n.d.). "Basic Principles of Systems Thinking as Applied to Management and Leadership." http://www.systemic leadershipinstitute.org/systemic-leadership/theories/basic-principles-of-systems-thinking-as-applied-to-management-and-leadership-2/.

Katzenbach, Jon R., and Douglas K. Smith. *The Wisdom of Teams: Creating the High-Performance Organization.* Boston: Harvard Business Review Press, 2015.

Kozhevnikov, Maria, Michael Kozhevnikov, Chen Jiao Yu, and Olesya Blazhenkova. "Creativity, Visualization Abilities, and Visual Cognitive Style." *British Journal of Educational Psychology* 83, no. 2 (2013): 196–209. DOI: 10.1111/bjep.12013.

Lakey, Chad E., Michael H. Kernis, Whitney L. Heppner, and Charles E. Lance. "Individual Differences in Authenticity and Mindfulness as Predictors of Verbal Defensiveness." *Journal of Research in Personality* 42, no. 1 (2008): 230–38.

Lamberg, T. D. and J. A. Middleton. "Design Research Perspectives on Transitioning from Individual Microgenetic Interviews to a Whole-Class Teaching Experiment." *Educational Researcher*, 38, no. 4 (2009): 233–245. http://dx.doi.org/10.3102/0013189X09334206.

Lamberg, Teruni. *Leaders Who Lead Successfully: How to Generate and Communicate for Innovation.* Lanham, MD: Rowman and Littlefield, 2018.

Lamberg, Teruni. *Whole Class Mathematics Discussions: Improving In-Depth Mathematical Thinking and Learning.* Boston: Pearson Higher Ed, 2012.

Lave, Jean, and Etienne Wenger. "Legitimate Peripheral Participation in Communities of Practice." *Supporting Lifelong Learning* 1 (2002): 111–26.

Lionni, Leo. *Fish Is Fish*, first edition. New York: Penguin Random House, 1974.

Louis, Barron. "Authentic Leadership and Mindfulness Development through Action Learning." *Journal of Managerial Psychology* 31, no.1 (2016): 296–311. DOI: 10.1108/JMP-04-2014-0135.

Lubart, Todd I. "Models of the Creative Process: Past, Present and Future." *Creativity Research Journal* 13, nos. 3–4 (2001): 295–308.

Maxwell, John. *How Successful People Think: Change Your Thinking, Change Your Life.* New York: Center Street, 2011.

———. *21 Irrefutable Laws of Leadership: Follow Them and People Will Follow You.* Nashville, TN: Thomas Nelson, 2007.

Morsing, Mette, and Majken Schultz. "Corporate Social Responsibility Communication: Stakeholder Information, Response and Involvement Strategies."

Business Ethics: A European Review 15, no. 4 (2006): 323–38. DOI: 10.1111/j.1467-8608.2006.00460.x.

Nagji, Bransi, and Geoff Tuff. "Managing Your Innovation Portfolio." *Harvard Business Review* 90, no. 5 (2012): 66–74.

Nathan, Mitchell J., and Karen Koellner. "A Framework for Understanding and Cultivating the Transition from Arithmetic to Algebraic Reasoning." *Mathematical Thinking and Learning* 9, no. 3 (2007): 179–92.

Pisano, Gary. "You Need an Innovation Strategy." *Harvard Business Review* (June 2015): https://hbr.org/2015/06/you-need-an-innovation-strategy.

Prentice, William. "Organizational Culture: Understanding Leadership." *Harvard Business Review* (January 2004): https://hbr.org/2004/01/understanding-leadership.

Sapp, D. David. "The Point of Creative Frustration and the Creative Process: A New Look at an Old Model." *The Journal of Creative Behavior* 26, no. 1 (1992): 21–28.

Vellera, Cyrielle, and Marie-Laure Gavard-Perret. "A Better Understanding of the Role and Underlying Mechanism of Stimulating Mental Imagery in Improving the Creativity of "Ordinary" Users." *Recherche et Applications en Marketing* (English edition) 31, no. 3 (2016): 111–30.

Wallas, George. *The Art of Thought*. Kent, England: Solis Press, 1926; reprinted, 2014.

About the Author

Teruni Lamberg is currently associate professor of mathematics education at the University of Nevada, Reno. She received her doctorate in mathematics education at Arizona State University in 2001 and completed a post-doctorate at Vanderbilt University. She is the author of *Whole Class Mathematics Discussions: Improving In-Depth Mathematical Thinking and Learning* and coauthor of *Smarter Balanced: Grade 3*. She is the principal investigator of the Nevada Mathematics Project.

She led a statewide initiative aimed at improving mathematics education for children through teacher training as well as researching the process of doing this. Her work has impacted more than 12,500 students in Nevada and involved collaborating with an interdisciplinary team made up of mathematicians, math educators, scientists, cognitive scientists, the Nevada Department of Education, Regional Professional Development Program Trainers, and every school district in Nevada. Leadership skills were critical in making this project a success, and therefore, she spent many years studying business literature. This project is now formalized as an institutional initiative with the backing of the Nevada governor's office and the State Superintendents Board of Nevada. It is now a permanent initiative of the college. (See http://www.unr.edu/education/centers/nevada-mathematics-project.)

Lamberg has also held many other leadership positions. She served twice as chair of the Psychology of Mathematics Education organization for the Northern American chapter (United States, Canada, and Mexico), a prestigious mathematics education research organization. She serves as the program coordinator for the STEM master's and doctoral programs at the University of Nevada, Reno. She is the director of the Nevada Mathematics Project Initiative.

www.ingramcontent.com/pod-product-compliance
Lightning Source LLC
Chambersburg PA
CBHW021602210326
41599CB00010B/566